JEAN SIBELIUS'S
VIOLIN CONCERTO

Oxford KEYNOTES

Series Editor   KEVIN C. KARNES

Oxford KEYNOTES

JEAN SIBELIUS'S
Violin Concerto

TINA K. RAMNARINE

OXFORD
UNIVERSITY PRESS

Oxford University Press is a department of the University of Oxford. It furthers
the University's objective of excellence in research, scholarship, and education
by publishing worldwide. Oxford is a registered trade mark of Oxford University
Press in the UK and certain other countries.

Published in the United States of America by Oxford University Press
198 Madison Avenue, New York, NY 10016, United States of America.

Library of Congress Control Number: 2020936082
ISBN 978-0-19-061153-8 (hbk.)
ISBN 978-0-19-061154-5 (pbk.)

9 8 7 6 5 4 3 2 1

Paperback printed by Marquis, Canada
Hardback printed by Bridgeport National Bindery, Inc., United States of America

Series Editor's
INTRODUCTION

O XFORD KEYNOTES REIMAGINES THE canons of Western music for the twenty-first century. With each of its volumes dedicated to a single composition or album, the series provides an informed, critical, and provocative companion to music as artwork and experience. Books in the series explore how works of music have engaged listeners, performers, artists, and others through history and in the present. They illuminate the roles of musicians and musics in shaping Western cultures and societies, and they seek to spark discussion of ongoing transitions in contemporary musical landscapes. Each approaches its key work in a unique way, tailored to the distinct opportunities that the work presents. Targeted at performers, curious listeners, and advanced undergraduates, volumes in the series are written by expert and engaging voices in their fields, and will therefore be of significant interest to scholars and critics as well.

In selecting titles for the series, Oxford Keynotes balances two ways of defining the canons of Western music: as lists of works that critics and scholars deem to have articulated key moments in the history of the art, and as lists of works that comprise the bulk of what consumers listen to, purchase, and perform today. Often, the two lists intersect, but the overlap is imperfect. While not neglecting the first, Oxford Keynotes gives considerable weight to the second. It confronts the musicological canon with the living repertoire of performance and recording in classical, popular, jazz, and other idioms. And it seeks to expand that living repertoire through the latest musicological research.

Kevin C. Karnes
Emory University

CONTENTS

ABOUT THE
COMPANION WEBSITE

www.oup.com/us/jsvc

Oxford University Press has created a website to accompany *Jean Sibelius's Violin Concerto* that features a variety of related multimedia materials, including audio clips and additional texts that extend the discussion on Sibelius's nature-based aesthetics, the Sibelius violin concerto, and issues around violin pedagogy. Many of these resources are integral to the volume itself or provide needed and useful context. As with all of the websites for Oxford Keynotes volumes, the reader is encouraged to take advantage of this valuable online information to expand their experience beyond the print book in hand. Examples available online are indicated in the text with Oxford's symbol [⏵]

ACKNOWLEDGMENTS

M Y RESEARCH HAS BEEN assisted by the remarkable guidance of staff at the Sibelius Museum Archive in Turku, Finland. I would like to extend particular gratitude to Sanna Linjama-Mannermaa for alerting me to relevant archive materials and photographic images. I also thank Johannes Brusila for sending me bibliographic material, which was difficult to locate, and Rutger Helmers for sharing information about violinists from all around Europe who visited or worked in Russia during the nineteenth century. The musician Timo Alakotila sent me the score of his prelude, commissioned for a 2019 BBC Proms performance of Sibelius's violin concerto with Pekka Kuusisto as soloist. Petra Piiroinen sent a photograph of the violinist Pekka Kuusisto from the collection of Our Festival in Finland, and Jelle Pieter de Boer sent his documentary photograph of the violinist Ida Haendel. I thank them all for their permission to reproduce these materials in this book. My research benefited from discussions with various musicians, and I am also grateful that Sophia Ramnarine kindly interviewed Kuusisto for this project and that Kevin C. Karnes, editor of the Oxford Keynotes series, read drafts of this volume and offered highly insightful comments.

JEAN SIBELIUS'S
VIOLIN CONCERTO

CHAPTER 1

SIBELIUS AS VIOLINIST
AND COMPOSER

I want so much to learn to play the violin.

Jean Sibelius, 1881

JEAN SIBELIUS WANTED TO be a master of the violin, not just to play it. This was why the Finnish music scholar Ilmari Krohn believed that Sibelius's Violin Concerto in D Minor, op. 47, was the composer's most intimate self-confession.[1] As Sibelius was crafting it, he was already a public figure, on the threshold of becoming Finland's most prominent voice, and later on a historical icon. In time, the violin concerto would bolster his global reputation by becoming one of the most beloved examples of its kind in the repertoire. All this still lay ahead as he worked carefully on the concerto that revealed his deepest musical aspirations. He thought about it as a violinist and as a composer, inspired by earlier contributions to the genre to offer new ways of thinking about virtuosity. The concerto demands

Jean Sibelius's Violin Concerto. Tina K. Ramnarine, Oxford University Press (2020). © Oxford University Press.
DOI: 10.1093/oso/9780190611538.001.0001

considerable skills from its soloists, many of whom underline its virtuosity in expressive terms. Maud Powell, for example, the violinist from Illinois who gave its American premiere in 1906, described how she became interested in the work on seeing the first theme. It "thrilled" her, and as she read through the movements, she thought that the concerto would "go beautifully."[2] Over a century after it was first performed, the Russian violinist Maxim Vengerov proclaimed, "This is beauty," when describing the concerto's opening declamation (⊙ see audio-visual example 1.1 on the website).[3]

Beauty as a philosophical discourse rests on aesthetic considerations, which are often articulated in terms of the relations between the symbolic and the social. For the German philosopher Georg Wilhelm Friedrich Hegel, these relations have a metaphysical dimension: beauty is the divine disclosed, and it is a universal form of a "self-unfolding idea."[4] Hegel suggests that art is a mode of perception and instruction with the purpose of revealing truth through its beauty. The purpose of art is immense. Art's beauty, its expressivity, reconciles the oppositions between inner subjective emotion and external phenomena, and it enables us to achieve our greatest fulfillment as humans, because it helps us to reimagine our relations to both each other and the natural world.[5] Beauty depends on labor; a work of art requires practice, skill, and "reflection on the mode of its productivity."[6]

What is the labor of virtuosity? Asking this question invites a new paradigm for virtuosity in the twentieth- and twenty-first centuries, which takes into account effort, rather than only extending nineteenth-century ideas about magical capacity or innate talent. Sibelius's violin concerto shows that virtuosity takes many forms across a spectrum from compositional imagination to creative performance. For the virtuoso violinist, labor hinges on two axes: repetitive practices in the cultivation of skill and the immediacy and creativity of communicative displays within public spheres. These are the intersecting axes of musical training and musical events, of practices behind the scenes and on stages. The latter links most closely with political action, drawing on Hegel's notion of art as a way of reimagining human relationships. The Russian writer Leo Tolstoy also believed that art serves a sociopolitical function by building social relationships, although he disagreed with Hegel's views on beauty and truth. For Tolstoy, the purpose of laboring over art (including the years spent in developing rapid finger movement on a musical instrument) is to build empathy by communicating feeling. Artistic labor has a moral dimension because "every work of art causes the receiver to enter into a certain kind of relationship both with him who produced, or is producing, the art, and with all those who, simultaneously, previously, or subsequently, receive the same artistic impression."[7] Tolstoy valued sincerity over beauty, since, in his view, the latter was a highly subjective aesthetic judgment.

Audiences are witnesses to the labor of virtuosity, to the spectacles of skill that are full of risk because of the unpredictability of live performance. The bravura tradition of Sibelius's time gave rise to the figure of the celebrity virtuoso, upon whom audiences concentrated their romantic ideals of heightened emotional experiences and aesthetic appreciation. One nineteenth-century legacy is seeing the virtuoso as a kind of magician, as the recipient of a divine and diabolical gift, as epitomized by the mythical image of the "demonic" violinist Niccolò Paganini.[8] The violinist Leopold Auer writes about the virtuoso as a "sorcerer" with a bow as a wand, who strives to give interpretative nuance through dynamics, timbre, and tempo to notes on a page.[9] This vision of sorcery is focused entirely on musical concerns. Its allusion to communication between the virtuoso and the audience is not the same as that found in Hegel's or Tolstoy's discussions of the sociopolitical purpose of works of art.

Sibelius began to sketch the violin concerto when he was in Italy, home to the workshops of some of the most famous luthiers, the virtuosos of instrument manufacture, including Stradivarius, Guarneri, and Amati. The work was premiered in 1904. Sibelius worked further on it the following year, largely prompted by his habit of compositional revision. As he polished its musical ideas for structural coherence, he drew on his specialist knowledge of the instrument's technical capacities, leading to an integration of his performance and compositional practices. His friend Baron Axel Carpelan, a fellow violinist who hoped Sibelius would compose this concerto, was the basis for a fictional protagonist of a novel, who described the sounds of the violin as "animal sinews forced to labor, and to utter shrieked protests."[10] In fact, the violinist Viktoria Mullova spoke about trying to play Sibelius's violin concerto using gut strings, those made from the material that the fictional Carpelan called "animal sinews," but they did not work for the fast passages of the third movement (⊙ see audio-visual example 1.2 on the website).[11] Sibelius described his own creative processes in terms of a battle in a letter he sent to Carpelan in April 1903.[12]

The violin continued to be a primary medium for Sibelius's musical thinking even when a tremor stopped him from playing in later life. There was a tactile dimension to his compositional imagination that stemmed from his training as a violinist. Jussi Jalas, his son-in-law and a conductor, observed Sibelius sitting at home in the library, and he testified to the kind of craft that must have absorbed the composer years earlier as he finalized the concerto at his writing desk in Ainola (Aino's abode), the family household. He commented that Sibelius fingered the "imaginary neck of a fiddle" and that his "hand shifted into positions, his fingers made as if to produce double-stops, and tried to form themselves into fingerings for melodic lines, which in his mind actually sounded like a violin playing."[13]

Another medium for Sibelius's musical thinking was the forest environment. The forest is part of Finnish national mythology as illustrated in the epic the *Kalevala*, which influenced Sibelius's works, notably his last composition, the symphonic poem *Tapiola* (1926). In this mythology, nature itself is divine. Nature and divinity are related, likewise, in neighboring Norse mystical tradition. Thor, for example, is the god of thunder, storms, and oak trees. Sibelius's musical and ecological thought was based on understanding nature as a "pantheistic eternity."[14] General reception to his works was confined to landscape imagery, which was fueled by Sibelius's declarations about the importance of the forest to his compositional processes, although these were rooted in a sacred understanding of the natural environment. His descriptions of compositional labor as a divine exercise invoked the mystical elements of Hegel's philosophies on beauty. In referring to his Fifth Symphony in E Flat Major (op. 82) in a diary entry of April 10, 1915, he wrote, "It is as if God . . . had thrown down mosaic pieces from the floor of the heavens and asked me to put them back as they were. Perhaps that is a good definition of composition—perhaps not?"[15] The musical inspiration Sibelius gained in the forest is contrary, however, to Hegel's views on the natural world as an external phenomenon and on the origins of an artistic work in "the territory of the spirit," which is a realm that presides over nature.[16] Sibelius's reverence for the natural environment combined with a phenomenological aesthetics of timbre that was enriched by his synesthesia, a neurological condition that caused him to experience sound as color and color as sound.[17] Bird and violin timbres were part of an intertwined sonic ecology in his musical imagination. Nature ideas appeared in the sketches for the concerto, with images of a sunrise and altered slur markings made to depict seagulls.[18] Levas, his personal secretary whom he appointed in his later life, observed that "it was not only in music that notes and tonalities were to be heard. They were about everywhere. . . . Speaking as an old violinist, Sibelius said that the bullfinch 'double-stopped.' "[19]

The human appears as one of nature's many sonic actors in this description. Sibelius's attunement to the diversity of nature's sonic actors began with his early composition *Vattendroppar* (*Water Droplets*, 1875), for violin and violoncello playing pizzicato. As a child, Sibelius conducted an ensemble of animals, of anthropomorphic musicians, in a demonstration of cross-species musical creativity. He wrote to his uncle Pehr that while playing on a rock he imagined its slope was an orchestra: "The crows were the oboes, the magpies the bassoons, the sea gulls the clarinets, the thrushes the violas, the chiffchaffs the violins, the pigeons the violoncellos, the pine thrushes the flutes, the cock on the farm the concert master, and the pig the percussionist."[20] These childhood impressions were his "precious inheritance" and an "inexhaustible source of inspiration."[21] Sibelius listened to the call of the crane as "the leitmotiv" of his life.[22]

Notable violinists with whom he interacted shared his interests in this kind of creative listening. Auer urged his violin students to listen to nature to develop interpretative nuance. Nature is "ever changing, ever showing us some new mood, some new phase of her inexhaustible self," he writes, and it is "the fountain-head of variety in expression."[23] As creative listeners, too, we might hear the muted string sonorities of the concerto's opening bars as an evocation of forest sounds, or, as the violinist Raphael Bronstein suggests, the surface of a lake upon which the violin soloist floats, like a swan.[24] In Finnish oral tradition, the forests and the lakes came into being through the singing of a mythical hero. Listening to the beginning of the concerto through these images transports the listener to Sibelius's sacred landscapes.

At the moment when Sibelius began to compose his concerto, and before the family had moved to the artistic community around Lake Tuusula to escape the distractions of nearby Helsinki, he wrote of trying to establish an appropriate working routine, planning changes to his compositional processes: "More at the writing-table—less with the piano. Yet, I once wanted to become a violin virtuoso, and this 'performing' element always takes such strange forms within me."[25] Composing and performing were integrated processes in his musical imagination, as Aino, his wife, mentioned in a letter to Carpelan in 1904. She described Sibelius's routine as he worked on the violin concerto:

> He has so many ideas forcing their way into his mind that he becomes quite literally dizzy. He's awake night after night, plays wonderful things, and can't tear himself away from the marvellous music he plays—there are so many ideas that one can't believe it is true, all of them so rich in possibilities for development, so full of life.[26]

They were so full of life that he continued to work with those ideas even after the concerto's premiere in February 1904. Sibelius began the revision process during a stay in Berlin from January to March 1905, and he wrote to Aino that he was "improving the Concerto quite a lot."[27] He also reported that the "first movement makes me conflicted. The others were just so clear to me."[28] Indeed, as the musicologist Timo Virtanen pointed out, the solo part and formal design of the first movement were the most thoroughly revised parts of the concerto, although the third movement was shortened considerably.[29] Sibelius simplified the balance between soloist and orchestra. He originally scored the violin solo beginning at the end of measure 53 in the first movement, for example, with a string and timpani accompaniment, but he replaced those instruments in the final version with a timpani tremolo accompanying the soloist for five measures before dwindling into silence.

By the summer of 1905, Sibelius had completed the work. He withdrew the first version of the concerto after its premiere. Later, the original score was retrieved and the first version was recorded (with Leonidas Kavakos, the winner of the 1985 Sibelius Violin Competition, as the soloist). This recording helps audiences understand some of the working processes of Sibelius's musical imagination, the ways in which he tightened the structure of the concerto and pruned its melodic ideas.[30] The musicians involved in this retrieval project asserted that future performers and audiences would decide whether or not to circulate the first version further. Both versions were published as part of the critical edition project looking closely at the primary sources, the *Jean Sibelius Works*.

Sibelius's violin concerto has held an important place in the public sphere since its premiere. It was performed by virtuoso violinists in Finland, Russia, and central Europe from the early twentieth century onward. It formed part of the core repertoire of Russian violinists who migrated to America at the time of the Russian Revolution in a new wave of the traveling virtuoso. It has been recorded by generations of virtuosos, from Jascha Heifetz, Ida Haendel, Ginette Neveu, and David Oistrakh to Sarah Chang, Pekka Kuusisto, and Maxim Vengerov, to name only a few examples.

This book tells the story of Sibelius's violin concerto. It is a story about virtuosity, tradition, and history. It is a story that moves beyond the notion of a great work to consider how a virtuoso concerto, which is a highly valued artifact, is located within specific cultural and historical contexts, as well as within the longer environmental histories of musical sounds (with which Sibelius demonstrated a strong affinity). By considering the concerto in relation to its broad contexts, the diverse ways in which violinists engage with this work (with reference to a few select examples), and the continuity of its transmission, we gain insights into how performing traditions are formed over time. The first part of the book concerns Sibelius as violinist and composer. It examines Sibelius's early musical training, the cultural and political contexts in which he worked, and the variety of compositional models on which he drew while working on his concerto, as well as his dialogues with prominent violinists in Helsinki. The second part of the book looks at Sibelius's concerto in relation to the formation of violin playing traditions. It focuses on the broader contexts of violin playing styles, musical transmission (especially through conservatory education), recordings as historical documents, and the violinists whose life stories are connected in various ways with Sibelius and his concerto. This book draws on insights from scholars, archival sources, accounts by violinists, biographies of the composer, and Sibelius's own words as recorded in the literature.

Three points can be outlined at the outset. First, since Sibelius has become such a towering figure in Finnish music, it is worth emphasizing that many other individuals are a part of the story of his violin concerto. Key figures emerge in the story because of their influence as pedagogues and their recorded interpretations. Auer, who taught at the St. Petersburg Conservatory, is one example; another is one of Auer's students, Heifetz, whose 1935 recording with the London Philharmonic revealed the concerto's merits in the hands of a violinist able to meet its challenges. Second, cross-genre interactions inform our perspectives on the transmission of performing traditions.

Connections between art, folk, and klezmer violin performing traditions were part of early twentieth-century musical life in northern Europe and the Russian Empire. These connections underlined Sibelius's diverse musical interests, which were supported by international travel and an intellectual outlook that was shaped by the Finnish tradition of comparative scholarship. The high status of comparative scholarship in Finland enabled artistic attitudes toward cultural practices to go beyond the limitations of Hegel's Eurocentric views on the importance of art as a privilege held by Europeans.[31] Comparative scholarship looked across geographic borders and encouraged global thinking. Thus, Sibelius thought about music in, for example, China and India, as well as in Finland, Russia, and central Europe.[32] Third, Sibelius lived through a period of industrialization, institutionalization, and technological innovation. But his retreat into the forest promotes contemporary ecological interpretations of his works. Together, these three points—that the work was shaped by the contributions of many individuals, that cross-genre practices informed Sibelius's thinking, and that concern for nature animated his creative imagination—overlap throughout this exploration of his violin concerto.

Jean Sibelius (1865–1957) was born in Hämeenlinna, a military town in Finland, which was then an autonomous Grand Duchy of the Russian Empire, in the year that Tolstoy began writing *War and Peace* and in the final stages of the American Civil War. In time, Sibelius became a musical chronicler of Finnish life on an epic scale, as Tolstoy had become a literary one for Russia. By the 1930s, Sibelius was one of the most popular composers among American audiences, and the middle section of his *Finlandia*, his most well-known patriotic work, had also become known as an American hymn. His earliest years, though, were shaped by the sounds of Russian military bands of brass, woodwinds, and drums, which paraded through his hometown and impressed a young Sibelius, who drew a sketch of one such display of imperial power for his grandmother and aunt.[33]

The 1860s saw a period of intense European nation-building projects and rising nationalism in Russia's provinces, including Poland, Estonia, and Latvia. This was a period of imperial competition between the great powers of Russia and Britain. British officials considered Russia's expansion into Central Asia as a threat to British India as they observed the occupation of Turkestan in 1864, then of Tashkent and Samarkand, followed by Khiva and Bukhara, most of which became Russian protectorates.[34] To the south of Bukhara was Afghanistan, a British protectorate. Russian imperial administration was closer to the French model than the British one; a military hierarchy governed Russia's territories, but elected officials took charge of local administrative processes. A new turn in Russian imperialism based on Russification policies followed the Polish insurrection of 1863, although Britain, France, and Austria demanded that Russia grant the Poles concessions. By 1878, when pan-Slavic insurgency in the Balkans led to the creation of Bulgaria, it was Germany that appeared as the predominant power in Europe. Russia turned its attention to Central Asia and to railway building.[35]

By the 1860s, the Finnish legislature, the Diet, was already an important state body dealing with internal constitutional, legal, and political matters, and Tsar Alexander II opened its 1863 meeting in Helsinki. An imperial need to move troops quickly led to a rail connection between Helsinki and Hämeenlinna. Trains are linked with empire building, modernity, industrialization, and labor. In Juhani Aho's novel *Rautatie* (*The Railway*, first published in 1884), an agricultural laborer learns that trains are "the iron road's horses that eat firewood while running."[36] Trains facilitated new performance circuits. Several musicians visited Hämeenlinna, including the violinists Gerhard Brassin, Anton Sitt, and the German child prodigy August Wilhelmj, who had become a student of the violinist and composer Ferdinand David in Leipzig on Franz Liszt's recommendation that he was the "future Paganini."[37] Wilhelmj became Richard Wagner's first violinist in the original Bayreuth Orchestra, and he was appointed professor of violin at the Guildhall School of Music and Drama in London in 1894.[38]

The Russian military presence in Hämeenlinna had important consequences for musical life. Gustaf Levander, the former Russian bandmaster of the Onegan regiment, gave music lessons to the town's children. Sibelius began studying with him in 1881 and was a member of a student orchestra that Levander established, as well as of a string quartet in which his teacher played the viola.[39]

Taking his earliest musical steps, Sibelius wrote this to his uncle Pehr on June 19, 1881:

I want so much to learn to play the violin and, in the event you let me, [I will] begin to take lessons from Music Director Levander in Tavestehus [Hämeenlinna in Swedish] next fall; kindly bring the violin which Aunt mentioned when you come here next time, please. True, I do have a violin, but I loaned it to one of my schoolmates, Karl Stenroth, who is poor and has a good talent for music, and I don't have the heart to take it away from him.[40]

Pehr gave Sibelius a violin that his brother, a sea captain, had acquired in a market in St. Petersburg. It is attributed to the seventeenth-century Austro-Germanic luthier Jacob Stainer. Sibelius played this violin for the rest of his performing career. His granddaughter Satu Jalas inherited it. She plays it on a 2014 recording of Sibelius's music performed on his own instruments, recorded at his home in Ainola.[41]

Playing music with his siblings was an important part of Sibelius's musical development (see photograph 1.1). On entering the Helsinki Music Institute (later renamed the Sibelius Academy of Music, and now part of the University of the Arts Helsinki), Sibelius studied with the Russian violinist Mitrofan Wasilieff (see photograph 1.2), who turned Sibelius's attention to works by French violinists (Rudolphe Kreutzer, Jacques Féréol Mazas, Jacques-Pierre Rode), Italian violinists (Giovanni Battista Viotti), and Belgian violinists (Henri François Vieuxtemps, Charles Auguste de Bériot, Alexandre-Joseph Artot). Bériot had published his famous *Méthode de Violon* in 1858 in Paris, and a Russian edition followed in 1870. It was an important text for Russian violinists. It emphasized solfège, performance technique, stylistic knowledge, and technical applications to realize the

PHOTOGRAPH 1.1   Trio of the Sibelius siblings: Jean Sibelius (1865–1957;
violin), Linda Sibelius (1863–1932; piano), and Christian
Sibelius (1869–1922; cello) at the spa casino in the
Finnish town Loviisa, where they used to play during the
summertime. Photograph by Natalia Linsén (1844–1919).
Reproduced with permission from the Sibelius Museum/
Stiftelsen för Åbo Akademi, Finland.

violin's expressive potential. As Bériot explained, "Feverish
striving for the development of technique . . . very often
takes the violin away from its truest and noblest task—to
imitate the human voice."[42]

Sibelius wrote letters to his uncle outlining his violin
studies. On September 17, 1885, he wrote this about his violin professor, Wasilieff: "He has the best references from
Rubinstein and has been a violinist in the imperial court
quartet. It probably takes a while before I understand
his method, but the work goes well."[43] By October 28, he
was able to report, "My playing is developing quite rapidly. In this month I have learned as much as I previously
learned in a year. My teacher, Wasilieff, is very pleased with

PHOTOGRAPH 1.2   The violin teacher Mitrofan Wasilieff (seated, *center*) with six students at the Music Institute of Helsinki (ca. 1885–86). From *left*: Elin Augusta Wärnhjelm (née Lönnblad), an unidentified girl, Jean Sibelius, Mitrofan Wasilieff, Anna Tigerstedt, Agnes Tschetschulin, and Gunnar Bergroth. Reproduced with permission from the Sibelius Museum/Stiftelsen för Åbo Akademi, Finland.

me. . . . Wasilieff is the son of music professor Wasilieff in Berlin. He is very talented and plays with fire and life, and possesses a colossal technique."[44] In the same letter, Sibelius noted that Wasilieff played a Stradivarius violin.

On November 14 of that year, Sibelius informed his uncle about a performance opportunity: "The purpose is to get rid of my stage fright, which a soloist must not suffer from."[45] At this time, he was studying Viotti's Concerto in G Major and Rode's Concerto in A Minor. A year later, he performed Bériot's seventh concerto, writing to his uncle about his new interpretation: "It has to be played in an entirely different manner than I have played before. You see, I played it too much in the classical way, heavily and correctly. Instead, it should sound brilliant and free, almost like an improvisation."[46] At this time, he began to study the compositions of Vieuxtemps, and he worked on scales and exercises to improve his tone. By September 27, 1887, Sibelius was studying Felix Mendelssohn's violin concerto and Rode's études with a newly appointed teacher, Hermann Csillag,[47] and he was looking forward to working on Ludwig van Beethoven's Romance in F Major (op. 50),[48] which he would perform as a soloist with the Academic Orchestra in March 1889.[49] Sibelius applied for a music scholarship with the support of the institute's director, Martin Wegelius. Sibelius cited Wegelius's comments in a letter to his uncle in March 1886: "Jean Sibelius, enrolled since the 15th of September at the Music Institute, has mainly studied violin performance and music theory there and made great progress in both subjects, and he has distinguished himself by his exceptional musical talent, particularly by an outstanding gift for the violin."[50] Sibelius's achievements were indeed considerable. His performances of concertos by Viotti, David, Bériot, Vieuxtemps, and Mendelssohn show that he was already an accomplished violinist during his years of study.

Sibelius's final examinations were successful. He reported, "After I played my concert I was called back twice and the room rang out with applause. But when my composition (a string quartet in C-sharp minor) was presented, I was applauded and called back almost countless times. . . . My teacher Csillag gave me straight As in violin performance (in diligence, ability, progress); Martin Wegelius gave me the same in composition."[51] By the autumn, he was performing with his teacher—possibly Spohr's Duo for Two Violins (op. 67).[52]

Alongside his violin and composition studies, Sibelius played in the Academic Orchestra, in the Trade Society Orchestra, and in chamber music ensembles.[53] In March 1889, he performed Schumann's Piano Quartet in E-flat Major (op. 44) with Ferruccio Busoni (piano), Csillag (violin), Karl Fredrik Wasenius (viola), and Wilhelm Renck (cello).[54] By July 6 of that year, Sibelius had composed a violin sonata.[55] He had been studying composition with the composer and musicologist Wegelius and the composer and conductor Robert Kajanus, who championed Sibelius's works and, notably, recorded his first, second, third, and fifth symphonies, together with *Tapiola*, with the London Symphony Orchestra in the 1930s. Wegelius guided Sibelius to continue his studies in Berlin and Vienna, recommending him for a state scholarship. He commented on a "rare instinct and talent" and concluded that Sibelius's "formal skill is matched by a genuine musical impulse, a lively, inventive capacity together with a rich and distinguished fund of inspiration, and thus as a composer his future gives rise to the most promising hopes."[56] The Finnish senate awarded Sibelius a travelling scholarship of two thousand marks for further studies in composition and violin. Wegelius offered some parting advice in 1889:

No person with any common sense is going to endorse all your musical ideas. . . . You haven't yet learned to distinguish the wheat from the chaff, the gold from the dross, which can also glisten in the sunshine. You are in need of a good spring-clean in this respect and when you have had it you will feel the benefit. After that you can write again anything that you want to, but you will no longer write the first thing that comes into your head.[57]

Sibelius's studies (1889–90) in counterpoint with Albert Becker in Berlin provided the "spring-clean." Additionally, Sibelius attended many concerts. He went to hear Mozart's *Don Giovanni*. He traveled with Busoni to Leipzig to hear him playing Sinding's piano quintet with the Brodsky Quartet, after which he composed his own Piano Quintet in G minor.

Sibelius's fascination with Finnish folk materials grew in the context of his early transnational studies in Europe's art-music environments. He heard Kajanus's symphonic poem *Aino* in February 1890 in Berlin, a work that alerted him to the musical possibilities of Elias Lönnrot's compilation of folk-song texts that had become the Finnish national epic, the *Kalevala*. Later in that year, he moved to Vienna. Busoni had written a letter of recommendation for Sibelius to study with Brahms in that city, but Brahms was no longer teaching. Neither was Bruckner, whose Third Symphony in D Minor so impressed Sibelius. Hans Richter referred him to Robert Fuchs, and Wegelius wrote a letter of recommendation for Sibelius to study with Karl Goldmark, who was a celebrity after composing the opera *The Queen of Sheba*. During this time, Sibelius auditioned unsuccessfully for the Vienna Philharmonic, an outcome that marked the end of his professional ambitions as a violinist. It was in Vienna that he planned the symphonic work *Kullervo*

(1892), in which he set over two hundred lines from the *Kalevala*. Sibelius turned to this text repeatedly throughout his life. In the final entry of his personal diary, in 1944, he wrote, "What enormous musical possibilities the *Kalevala* offers."[58]

The Finnish musicologist Erik Tawaststjerna wondered what Sibelius's musical development might have been if he had studied with Rimsky-Korsakov in St. Petersburg instead of being guided by Wegelius to Austro-Germanic musical models.[59] Even though he did not study in St. Petersburg, Russian musical models, which were connected with French ones, offered him new means of tonal organization and symphonic syntax. By looking at these musical models, Sibelius refined his sense of harmonic language and learned a way of drawing on folk motives enabling him to balance "the lure of nationalism, the specific, and the self-consciously provincial on the one hand, and an interest in the abstract, the general, and the universal on the other."[60] This balance preoccupied early Sibelius biographers, who posed the question whether Sibelius should be regarded as a national or universal composer. The question derived from a concern to maintain the centrality of a particular kind of canon in which some composers were viewed as speaking for all humanity (they were universal) in contrast to others who only spoke for the nation in which they were located.

Questions about a composer's sphere of influence are political in intent. Hegel articulated ideas about universalism (applied to questions of musical value) in his influential text *Phenomenology of Spirit*, first published in 1807, which argued for the sociopolitical potential of a discipline (philosophy) to construct Plato's "ladder" in order to offer a vista of the phenomenological communion of all "conscientious" persons, meaning those acting from conscience.[61] This text led to his later reflections on art as historically embedded and on beauty's spiritual purpose, following a philosophical tradition of metaphysical enquiry. His ideas about the spiritual reconciliations that might emerge from an understanding of human moral differences informed nation-state projects of self-recognition across Europe. The philosopher and politician Johan Vilhelm Snellman (1806–81), one of the architects of Finnish society, was among the political thinkers Hegel influenced. Snellman wrote a doctoral thesis on Hegel, and he was appointed to the post of lecturer at the Imperial University in 1835. Later on, as a politician, he played a central role in fostering national self-consciousness and asserting cultural power as a route toward self-determination. In Finland, as elsewhere, the folk provided a category for thinking simultaneously about the universal and the local, as well as about cultural power. In the wake of Johann Gottfried Herder's intellectual interests in the folk, networks of scholars and artists all over Europe supported the ideal of human societies divided into nations that were determined by culture, territory, and language. This intellectual network was one reason why Sibelius undertook a study of folk traditions, which he valued highly.

The political context of the violin concerto could hardly have been more dramatic. Sibelius dreamed of violin virtuosity, and he worked on the concerto in the years of passive resistance, revolutionary activities, and a political assassination on the streets of Helsinki. The target of the assassination, which took place in 1904, was Nikolai Ivanovich

Bobrikov. He had been appointed in 1898 as Governor-General of Finland by Tsar Nikolai II, who ruled from 1894 to 1917. Nikolai's implementation of Russification policies led to new restrictions on the press and to the revision of school and university curricula, including the introduction of new historical textbooks. In 1899, Sibelius participated in a high-profile protest against these policies by composing *Music for the Press Celebrations* as part of a collaborative multimedia artwork for a gala evening at the Swedish Theatre in Helsinki. Its premiere exemplified the potential of art to turn spectators into conscious agents in the remaking of the political world.[62] The last tableau later became widely known as *Finlandia*. It asserted the contrast (political and musical) between Finland and Russia in international spectacles, notably the 1900 Paris World Exhibition, in which its performance (with the title *La Patrie*) offered a "counterproposal" to the 1889 Paris World Fair performance of Anton Rubinstein's fantasy *Rossiya*.[63]

Sibelius completed the violin concerto amid ongoing protests against Russia's borderland policy, complications around who would be the soloist, and a change of publisher. Europe was on the brink of the momentous geopolitical changes that were to come with the General Strikes, the First World War, the Russian Revolution, and, amid the turmoil, the Finnish Declaration of Independence. Musical performances on these political stages made Sibelius a "musical icon," because he developed the idea of what Finnish national music might sound like,[64] defining the sounds of self-determination and a new democratic politics.

The relations between the artist and the state are about how power is constructed within human societies. State formations and governance dominate political thought about power. It is also worth considering how power is constructed through expressive means. Thus the play between power and culture is a core question in cultural theory,[65] and virtuosity is one of its aspects as depicted in nineteenth-century imagery. The Romantic violin virtuoso was depicted as a hero, as a "symbol of military power," and violinists from Paganini to Spohr "wielded their bows like swords and commanded armies of orchestral musicians, inviting comparison with military leaders, ancient and modern."[66] While Paganini seemed to hold his bow like a sword, Joseph Bologne was in fact both a virtuoso violinist and a champion fencer.[67] Public perceptions of the nineteenth-century military-heroic virtuoso "permeated virtually every aspect of violin composition, performance, and reception, from the notes themselves to the symbolic meanings of performers and instruments."[68]

One consequence of military-heroic imagery is that the labor of virtuosity brings the economic and political dimensions of power into focus. Economics underpinned the new meanings that virtuosity acquired when Karl Marx's ideas about labor as the foundation of unequal sociopolitical relations were put to the test in the revolutionary action that unfolded only a few years after Sibelius composed the violin concerto. Marx reflected on the ownership that people hold over the means of their own production, their capacity, in other words, to control their labor (first published in *Capital: Critique of Political Economy*, in 1867).[69] In a draft manuscript written between 1862 and 1863 he suggested that labor "bestows on objects almost their whole value."[70] Marx focused on relationships based on exchanges between capital and wage labor. He made a distinction between the artist's relationships with the public and with an employer. In the former relationship, the identity of a performer as an "artist" is predominant. In the latter, the artist is a "productive worker" able to generate capital in the moment of a performance.[71] This means that the labor of virtuosity is not productive in itself; it becomes so in the hands of an entrepreneur who generates capital from it. Virtuosos who are dependent on an entrepreneur for capital are wage laborers, just like agricultural workers, without control over the means of their production. In the public sphere, however, they are artists, and their labor holds political potential.

The idea of the virtuoso's political potential builds on nineteenth-century philosophical discussion of the redemptive potential of civic action. Where there are moral uncertainties around the spaces of human action, the symbolism of virtuosity as powerful conveys the philosopher Friedrich Nietzsche's notion of music as magical, as a "saving sorceress" with Dionysian qualities (irrational and subjective) that transform a person's incapacity to act in the face of contemplating the absurdity of political will.[72] Redemption lies in the restoration of political action through music's magical qualities, according to this philosophy. In the twenty-first century, the sorcerer's skill is seen as resting on everyday speech, which is the kind of virtuosity that the Italian philosopher, Paolo Virno explores. He suggests virtuosity is the capacity not only of a highly-skilled musical performer but also of anyone who speaks, and that the virtuoso's purpose is to generate a social movement and a different kind of politics.[73] This is a contemporary perspective on virtuosity that is indebted to both nineteenth-century representation of the virtuoso violinist as a heroic figure and ideas about music's connection with political action. Virtuosity offers the possibility of social change by stirring political disobedience, according to Virno, and the idea is relevant when considering the historical protests taking place on Helsinki's streets as Sibelius finalized his concerto.

If there is sorcery in violin virtuosity—skill seen as a magical attribute—there is also the discipline of practice. Discipline lies in Marx's category of nonproductive labor, and it is willingly cultivated by virtuoso violinists because it develops (in Hegel's and Tolstoy's philosophical terms) an aesthetics of beauty and social relationships. Sibelius's long-term commitment to the violin was revealed in one of his diary entries. Sibelius wrote, as a fifty-year-old international celebrity, "Dreamt I was twelve years old and a virtuoso."[74]

CHAPTER 2

MUSICAL LIFE
IN HELSINKI (1880–1905)

A CONTEXT FOR SIBELIUS'S
VIOLIN CONCERTO

FINLAND'S POLITICAL GEOGRAPHY HAS fostered cultural exchanges amid military turmoil, including the Russo-Swedish wars. Finland was part of the Kingdom of Sweden for six centuries before it was ceded to the Russian Empire in 1809 following Russia's defeat of Sweden. It gained a new political status as the autonomous Grand Duchy of Finland within the Russian Empire. Shortly afterward, in 1812, the seat of government was transferred from Turku to Helsinki because of the latter's greater proximity to Russia. Helsinki, which was founded in 1550, became the new capital, and Tsar Alexander I commissioned Carl Ludvig Engel to redesign it architecturally. Engel, trained at the Berlin Bauakademie, wrote letters to his family about the boulders in Helsinki being "blasted away where the new streets will

Jean Sibelius's Violin Concerto. Tina K. Ramnarine, Oxford University Press (2020). © Oxford University Press.
DOI: 10.1093/oso/9780190611538.001.0001

be laid out" and about the "beautiful" city that was taking shape with its new university, senate, and Lutheran cathedral.[1] Its neoclassical architecture "symbolized a new era in the development of the country."[2]

Helsinki is at the crossroads of power in the north. It is part of transnational trading networks and artistic exchanges across the Baltic Sea region. It is, as the cultural historian Hannu Salmi observes, an important actor in a music history seen from the geographical perspectives of Finland, Sweden, and the Baltic states,[3] places that are no longer considered peripheral to musical centers such as Berlin and Vienna. Recent scholarship on networks, patterns of human mobility, and institutions has reshaped ideas about geographic relations between centers and peripheries, in which some places seemed to be more important than others. Places formerly regarded as centers are displaced to enable historical perspectives from other places to come to the forefront.

The foundations for Helsinki's music institutions were laid when an Academic Music Society was established in 1827.[4] It was supported by the university from 1828 onward.[5] In 1835, the composer-conductor from Hamburg Fredrik Pacius arrived in Helsinki (having served as a court musician in Stockholm) to take up an appointment as a music teacher at the Imperial Alexander University of Finland (the University of Helsinki after 1919). He was instrumental in organizing concerts, which featured Mozart's and Beethoven's symphonies as well as his own compositions, including the Violin Concerto in F-sharp Minor (1845). Pacius had studied with Louis Spohr, who emphasized "a singing violin tone and the expression of the inner qualities of music" above virtuosity alone.[6] He is celebrated today as the father of Finnish music and the composer of the national anthem, a setting of a poetic text by Johan Ludvig Runeberg, *Vårt land* (Swedish for "Our land," *Maamme* in Finnish). By the 1840s, student activities dominated urban life.[7] The university's concert hall rivaled other performance venues in the city and was filled for performances given by musicians such as the touring virtuoso Eugène Ysaÿe in 1883. The Helsinki Orchestra Association, established in 1882, promoted professional activity. Eminent figures such as the conductor, composer, and teacher Robert Kajanus, who worked with the Helsinki Philharmonic Orchestra, championed Sibelius's compositions.

Institutions provide the social apparatus for developing the practices of art music. Helsinki's musical institutions, namely, orchestras, choirs, and conservatories, had formed only shortly before Sibelius's birth. The conservatory is a training ground for the virtuoso, and its system of one-to-one teaching encourages the transmission of performance traditions through diverse musical lineages. For example, when Felix Mendelssohn accepted a post as conductor of the Gewandhaus Orchestra in Leipzig in 1842, he planned a new music conservatory in which orchestral players would teach their instruments. Mendelssohn appointed the concertmaster Ferdinand David to the post of professor of violin, and appointments for viola and violoncello followed in 1848 and 1853, respectively. The Berlin Conservatory opened in 1866 with Joseph Joachim as the violin professor. Anton Rubinstein founded the conservatory in St. Petersburg in 1862, where the professor of violin was the

Polish virtuoso Henryk Wieniawski, who had studied with the Belgian virtuoso Lambert Joseph Massart.

The mobility of musicians consolidated the conservatory as a principal institution for musical training, and it connected cities. St. Petersburg enjoyed a transnational scene with violinists from Italy arriving in the 1720s, then from France (including Pierre Rode and Pierre Baillot, who worked at the conservatory between 1803 and 1812) and, later on, from Germany. Tsar Alexander II approved the establishment of the Russian Musical Society in 1859. The emancipation of the serfs in 1861 also had implications for musical life. Serfs had served as professional musicians in the Russian courts, and music had been linked with aristocratic consumption rather than civic projects.[8] By the end of the nineteenth century, St. Petersburg had seen the emergence of a Russian virtuoso from a serf social background (Ivan Yefstafyevich Khandoshkin; see chapter 4), an orchestra, music societies, and a concert life that was linked to the wider European circuit.

Conservatory education in Finland began when Martin Wegelius established the Helsinki Music Institute (later the Sibelius Academy of Music) in 1882. He lectured there while working as a music critic and writing a comprehensive history of music. He had studied in Vienna, Leipzig, and Munich, and he encouraged German musical thought in Helsinki's music institutions. Wegelius's pedagogic interests contributed to a discourse on nationalism and universalism in music, and he introduced the German model of the musical association by founding an informal club, the Wagnerföreningen (Wagner Society), whose members included Kajanus and the composer and critic Karl Flodin.

Musical associations flourished in Finland and across the Baltic provinces, especially in Riga, due to strong German cultural influences. In 1876, Wegelius traveled to Bayreuth to hear Wagner's Ring Cycle. He wrote performance reviews for the Finnish press, which other festival visitors from the Baltic and Nordic countries (including Sibelius, in 1894) found informative. He promoted a view that Wagner was a universally significant composer, and he tried to write a book about him (which was not completed and remained unpublished). Wegelius's conservatory students were acquainted with his view that Wagner was the heir to the musical legacy of Bach and Beethoven,[9] the canon on which the notion of the universal rested.

Between 1880 and 1905, Wegelius; the Helsinki Philharmonic Orchestra; the conductors Kajanus, Armas Järnefelt, and Georg Schnéevoigt; the singer Aino Ackté; and, of course, Sibelius, among others, dominated the capital's musical life. Orchestral life flourished during this pre-independence period. It included community-based and amateur orchestras that formed across the country to perform Sibelius's symphonies, and which later provided the foundations for the further development of orchestral professionalism. By the 1880s, the world's cultural traditions were also on display in Helsinki. Australian indigenous, Indian, Ghanaian, and Sri Lankan performers, accompanied by boomerangs and elephants, performed in the city's circus and variety shows. Italian, Hungarian, and Spanish music was performed in Helsinki too.[10]

Kajanus, who had trained in Helsinki, Leipzig, and Paris, became a dominant musical figure by the 1880s because of his orchestral work. He conducted the Helsinki

Philharmonic Orchestra, which grew out of an orchestra he owned together with some local business investors, and which was hosted by the Helsinki Orchestra Association. Performances included the Finnish premiere of Beethoven's Ninth Symphony in D Minor (op. 125) in 1888. Regular orchestral concerts had become part of the city's musical life by the 1870s. Among other conductors, two figures contributed to broadening orchestral music's audiences. One was the German Jewish conductor of the Swedish Theater Orchestra, Nathan Barnet Emanuel. He organized promenade concerts based on performance models from London and Paris. The venues for these public concerts included parks and open-air restaurants. The other was the Czech conductor of the Helsinki Concert Orchestra, Bohuslav Hřímalý, who gave a series of performances between 1879 and 1882. The programs were varied, as in all European musical centers at this time, featuring a range of genres, "incidental music, overtures, symphonies, concertos, fantasias, orchestral suites, concert waltzes, gallops, marches and polkas, and other kinds of musical entertainment."[11] In an interview with the newspaper *Helsingin Sanomat* in 1932, Kajanus recounted that he was living in Dresden when he heard about the eighteen musicians in Hřímalý's orchestra and decided that he would return home to establish a new orchestra.[12] He assembled thirty-six musicians, many of them from Germany. The orchestra's rehearsal language was German, noteworthy since Kajanus was already negotiating financial support from the city in terms that were inflected by language politics.[13] In the next few years, he negotiated with Russian authorities to gain financial support for Finnish musical institutions and demonstrated astute political ability in navigating between the complexities of Finnish artistic nationalism and Russian liberal politics.[14] By 1885, Kajanus had set up his own orchestra school, and he appointed the violinist Anton Sitt as the orchestra's concertmaster, forbidding him to continue teaching for Wegelius at the music institute. This is illustrative of a "schism between the city's two leading musical personalities,"[15] though Wegelius and Kajanus reconciled, and the former invited the latter to a concert given by students at the institute in 1889. Wegelius's most outstanding student, Sibelius, was among the performers.[16]

Under Kajanus's direction, the Helsinki Philharmonic gave commercial "popular concerts" for the educated classes and "people's concerts" from 1888 onward, with the latter supported by municipal funding given because of public education policies stemming from Snellman's school reforms to develop a national society.[17] The distinction between popular and people's concerts was a legacy of class-based divisions in these reforms; the basic education provided in the common school was envisioned as helping the "lower classes find their proper niche in society," whereas the grammar school would "cultivate children of the higher classes according to their own calling."[18] In opposition to this class-based nationalism, others argued for a state-regulated common curriculum to ensure equality and social mobility for all Finns. Public interest in music education emerged in the context of these debates, and in 1907 the musicologist Otto Andersson was among those who argued for "the essential significance [that] musical art has in our life both at home and in school."[19]

Kajanus's orchestra continued to attract transnational membership. The cellist Georg Schnéevoigt, who had been working with the Hamburg Orchestra, enrolled in Kajanus's orchestra school and appeared as soloist in a performance of one of Haydn's cello concertos in 1895. By the end of 1896, there were sixty players in Kajanus's orchestra, and this might have been the last year that Sibelius played in the ensemble as a violinist. A European tour of 1900 (to Berlin and Paris, among other cities) increased the orchestra's local esteem (see photograph 2.1), which was augmented by solo appearances by the violinists Alexander Ziloti, Leopold Auer, and the former concertmaster, Wilhelm Burmester.[20]

By 1892, Sibelius shared Kajanus's status as one of the leading figures in Helsinki's concert life. His *Kalevala*-inspired compositions were indebted to Kajanus's compositional models and to Karelianism, a cultural movement that

PHOTOGRAPH 2.1   The orchestra of the Philharmonic Society of Helsinki rehearsing in the fire brigade's house in Helsinki before its tour to Paris in 1900. Robert Kajanus was conducting. Reproduced with permission from the Sibelius Museum / Stiftelsen för Åbo Akademi, Finland.

encouraged the study of vestiges of ancient folk heritage that survived in the eastern regions of Finland. Karelianism illustrated the intersections between cultural regeneration (the project of preserving and reviving folk traditions) and political innovation (based on nationalist philosophies). Sibelius's works, informed by his interests in art and folk traditions, had come to define musical nationalism in Finland by the end of the century. His creative practices were located within nineteenth-century cultural politics, and the works that drew on *Kalevala* themes in particular seemed to express explicit political intent. Even the tragic hero of *Kullervo* can be read within the moral frameworks of a community struggling for independent statehood.[21]

Sibelius's musical experiences were profoundly transnational. Between 1890 and 1931, he visited Berlin at least thirty-six times, almost annually, and it remained an important city for his professional activities. His works were published there, as well as in Leipzig. When Sibelius first went to study in Berlin, the city was emerging as the main center for Nordic modernism beyond the north. Henrik Ibsen, Edvard Munch, and August Strindberg also spent time there.[22] In addition, Sibelius noted philosophical affinities with his Russian counterparts, saying that he had been "guided by the very same principles of national individuality that distinguishes the music of the great Russian masters."[23] Artistic connections between Helsinki and St. Petersburg were facilitated by geographic proximity and by Kajanus's interest in Russian music (which meant that Alexander Glazunov, Rubinstein, Auer, Sergei Rachmaninoff, Vasiliy Safonov, and Ziloti visited Helsinki). In turn, Kajanus, Sibelius and Järnefelt visited

St. Petersburg as conductors. At Ziloti's invitation, Sibelius gave performances in Russia in 1906 and 1907, which critics acclaimed in the Russian press.[24]

Cross-border cultural interactions developed under complex political conditions. The promotion of Finnish music, especially in international contexts, became increasingly significant as concert life developed within Russia's sphere of political influence. Musical performances were included at the 1900 Paris World Exhibition, in which the Finnish Pavilion was constructed to display Finland's architectural innovations. Kajanus included extracts of Sibelius's works in the Helsinki Philharmonic Orchestra's programs. Sibelius thus became celebrated as a Finnish composer in a musical arena that had already seen the October 1893 French-Russian celebrations (Les Fêtes Franco-Russes) cementing a political alliance between imperial Russia and the French Third Republic through cultural means.[25] These performances drew attention to questions about policy and autonomy within the Russian Empire because of the distinction Parisian audiences drew between Finnish and Russian music.

International audience reception supported the politics of self-determination. Since the 1860s, Finland had resisted Russia's proposed extension of its Great Reforms to its borderlands on the basis of autonomy. The Russian governor-generals of Finland between 1855 and 1881 were favorably disposed toward Finnish interests, including support for extending the use of the Finnish language, which was promoted by the members of the Fennomania (Finnish-speakers') movement, who founded a political party and aspired to build a Finnish nation based on language and culture. Until the Bobrikov era, Finland's autonomy had benefitted from a brief period of Russian decentralization policies, which encouraged self-government and set the stage for liberal parliamentary democracy. From 1863 onward, the Finnish Diet had enacted legislation regarding freedom of worship, monetary independence, and a separate Finnish army. The Russian press had speculated on the dangers of Finnish separatism in the 1860s, but Russia's centralization policy, which was imposed on the Baltic provinces and Poland, did not apply to Finland.[26]

This political situation changed with the appointment of Governor-General Bobrikov in 1898. He attempted to establish Russian as the language of government, and he imposed new restrictions on the Finnish press. His policies were inflected by an emphasis on class divisions. He promised to give land to landless populations and granted special publication privileges to the Social Democrats, who were linked with class struggle in an international labor movement. He paid attention to the teaching of history and geography by urging revisions to textbooks and curricula, as well as by attempting to restrict the circulation of Runeberg's *Vårt Land*.[27] These attempts seemed irreconcilable with the original terms of constitutional protection and autonomy granted by Alexander I.[28] Late nineteenth-century debates about the relationship between Finland and Russia thus centered on the terms set around Russia's territorial acquisition of Finland.[29] Finnish nationalism gained momentum in this context. It brought the peasant class and the bourgeoisie together in a united national politics that emphasized constitutional rather than revolutionary aims across complex class alliances that had been made between peasants on one hand and élites on the other, across the Finnish-Russian border.[30] Revolutionary aims regarding rights issues that had led to the general strike in Russia and Finland in 1905 persisted, however, and Finnish national unity gave way to the civil war in the wake of independence.

Cultural exchanges nevertheless continued. In addition to his interests in the *Kalevala*, Sibelius read works by Russian authors, notably Tolstoy, Chekov, Pushkin, Gogol, and Turgenev, which were translated into Finnish and Swedish. Russian literature had become part of Finnish cultural life with the publication, beginning in 1876, of the Swedish-language literary journal *Finsk Tidskrift* (Finnish Journal), which published reviews of authors such as Tolstoy and Dostoevsky. The Finnish Theater staged plays by Russian authors, and the works of the Finnish playwright Aleksis Kivi were performed in St. Petersburg. In Finland, Tolstoy was especially popular by the end of the nineteenth century, and Finnish authors visited him at his home. The literary journal *Finlandia*, established in 1908, published both Finnish and Russian works. In turn, Finnish literature (including Swedish-language works) was translated into Russian. The Russian critic V. I. Golovin, for example, translated Runeberg's *Vårt Land* in 1902, just as Bobrikov was criticizing its wide circulation in Finland.

Even folk song research, the most nationally oriented of intellectual pursuits, was shaped by transnational trends. Folk song research in Finland developed in response to Lönnrot's *Kalevala*, and this work led to the coalescence of methodological and conceptual paradigms in Finno-Ugric studies, dominated by comparative, philological, and ethnographic approaches. These approaches were linked to a pan-European intellectual concern, particularly within ethnology and anthropology, with the human family's cultural characteristics and the connections between them. Research precedents for Helsinki-based scholars could be found in the Academy of Sciences in St. Petersburg, which had been an important center of Finno-Ugric studies between 1725 and 1860. The academy developed the most significant library and archive of fieldwork-based materials, which was used by the biggest group of scholars working together on Finno-Ugric topics. Research was published in Russian, Latin, German, and French to enable international exchanges. The contributions of individual scholars and Russia's development as a northern imperial force drove this intellectual center's undertakings, an enterprise that began when Peter the Great corresponded with Gottfried Wilhelm Leibniz about emulating the model of the German Academy of Sciences in Russia. This model included the development of ethnographic and linguistic research, surveys of Russia's natural resources and wildlife, and research on industrial technology in a project of scientific nationalism. Increased scientific rigor led to a new research protocol and large-scale projects on Finno-Ugric populations within the empire from 1780 onward, which furthered comparative and transnational perspectives.

By the end of the eighteenth century, Russian imperial scientific descriptions of the peoples within its territory had begun to enter into dialogues with Finnish investigation of language and cultural expression in the processes of national identification. Both research agendas were shaped by politics, but the dialogues between them were productive. The academy in St. Petersburg attempted to recruit

Finnish scholars to assist with further research, notably Gabriel Porthan in 1795, who declined on the grounds of health and age. By the beginning of the nineteenth century, scholarly interests had converged along the political lines of Russian knowledge about Russia and Finnish intellectual work as a part of nation-building in Finland. This culminated in Finland in 1835 with the literary output of Lönnrot (the first edition of the *Kalevala* was published in this year), the poet Johan Ludvig Runeberg, and the historian Anders Johan Sjögren who spent time working in St. Petersburg. Sjögren was guided by Herder's ideas on folk cultural expressions as he undertook extensive fieldwork from Russia across Karelia, Finland, the Sámi regions, and the Kola Peninsula. He fulfilled two research demands, one of which was to write a history for the Finnish people and the other of which was to produce documentation supporting Russian scientific priorities.[31] The scholar Julius Krohn pursued comparative ethnographic studies, researching cultural relationships across borders[32] and the nature-based beliefs of related Finnish peoples, including their musical practices.[33] His historical-geographic inquiry into folklore materials shaped the work of his sons, Kaarle, who focused on analysis of *Kalevala* type examples, and Ilmari, who contributed to folk song research and generated a classification system that informed European folk music research in the decades that followed.[34] Ilmari Krohn, who had trained as an organist at the Leipzig Conservatory in Germany, became a leading scholar in Finnish musicology. His work included a major study of Sibelius's symphonies.[35] In turn, this tradition of scholarship lent intellectual support to artistic fascination—including Sibelius's—with folk traditions. Disciplinary interests were, in short, a fundamental aspect of Helsinki's thriving musical life during the period.

In the 1890s, Krohn saw Sibelius as the musical articulator of the nation's struggles, and by 1945 he had published a programmatic meta-narrative for the symphonies, which Markus Mantere summarized in these terms: "*Kullervo* and the 1st Symphony depict the 'ancient time of legends,' the 2nd Symphony showing the eclipse of that time. The 3rd and 4th Symphonies depict 'the inner life of the human soul.' . . . Sibelius's last three symphonies . . . bring the northern, truly Finnish landscape to sound in seasons. The 5th is the symphony of spring, the 6th of summer, and the 7th of autumn."[36] His career traces the ongoing contemplation of music within national and pan-European frames beyond 1905. He was appointed in 1918 as the first professor of musicology at the Imperial Alexander University of Finland, and he participated in European musicological meetings where he presented papers on the *Kalevala* and folk music. His students Armas Launis, Otto Andersson, and Toivo Haapanen continued with Sibelius research, which he had established as an important field of study.

Although Sibelius crafted musical relationships, not social ones, we might recall nineteenth-century imageries of the triumphant, heroic violin virtuoso and Krohn's portrait of the composer as the musical voice of national struggles to read the political imaginary of the concerto in relation to cooperation and conflicts at the beginning of the twentieth century. The concerto was finalized in the wake of Bobrikov's policies. Class struggles were uniting peasants across territorial borders even as political figures resisted assimilation policies in Russia's imperial borderlands. Its premiere took place on the cusp of the political reform that implemented universal suffrage (giving all adult men and women the right to vote) and laid the foundations for Finland's modern democratic system. Helsinki was a city of political resistance and disturbance, erupting, as Sibelius finalized his concerto, in the general strike of 1905 (a precursor to the Finnish civil war, short and brutal, in 1918) that unleashed "an avalanche of new ideas," putting "the old conception of authority and of a patriarchal order" to the test, and activating the masses in the rise of socialist claims to equality.[37] Even though nationalist politics in Finland gained momentum during the late nineteenth century, Helsinki was a transnational and cosmopolitan city. Helsinki, like other European musical centers (Berlin, Paris, London, and St. Petersburg) was a city of musical encounter and exchange. Its musicians traveled across transnational musical circuits. The city's musical life, then and now, illustrates the multidimensionality of border-making practices, cultural production across states, and artistic activity amid geopolitical change.

CHAPTER 3

COMPOSING
THE VIOLIN CONCERTO

S IBELIUS'S COMPOSITIONS FOR VIOLIN demonstrate the social basis of creativity. His early compositions included duos and trios to play with his siblings and string quartets for the musicians with whom he played in Hämeenlinna. He composed around sixty violin works throughout his career, mostly short pieces, two serenades, and six humoresques. He began thinking about the violin concerto long before he completed it. One year after completing his Sonata for Violin and Piano in F Major (1889), Sibelius mentioned plans for a concerto in a letter to Aino. This work preoccupied him entirely to the extent that the composer and Sibelius biographer Nils-Eric Ringbom thought of him as "relatively unproductive" during this period of composing.[1] Tawaststjerna speculated that Sibelius

Jean Sibelius's Violin Concerto. Tina K. Ramnarine, Oxford University Press (2020). © Oxford University Press.
DOI: 10.1093/oso/9780190611538.001.0001

adopted a strategy of procrastination through excessive socializing, in order to avoid "getting to grips with the concerto."[2] Sibelius was enthusiastic, albeit daunted by his wish to write a work for the kind of virtuoso he had imagined himself becoming just a few years before. He composed the work with preceding musical models in his mind, influences from performers, and reflections on critical comments, including his own self-criticism.

MODELS

The existing violin concerto repertoire, including examples by Beethoven, Brahms, Tchaikovsky, and Mendelssohn, provided Sibelius with obvious musical models. Another model may have been the violin concerto composed in 1897 by Ferruccio Busoni, who taught at the Helsinki Music Institute and was Sibelius's friend and mentor, but not formally one of his teachers. Sibelius certainly attended a performance of Busoni's violin concerto in Berlin, later on, in 1914, with Josef Szigeti as the soloist.[3] Although critics once dismissed Busoni's compositional skills, overshadowed as they were by his reputation as a prominent virtuoso pianist,[4] more recent reviews regard his concerto as an accomplished work.[5] It is a lyrical example that includes much arpeggio and scalar writing, and it was dedicated to the Dutch violinist Henri Petri, who was a student of Joseph Joachim, one of the most prominent violinists of his time and the musician whom Brahms consulted when composing his own violin concerto. When Busoni first met Sibelius in Helsinki, in 1888, they met regularly to talk about music. They continued to discuss composition, orchestration, experiments with sound, and timbre until nearly the end of Busoni's life.

Sibelius knew Mendelssohn's concerto intimately, having performed it himself as a soloist, and he learned much from the structural innovations of this model. In both Mendelssohn's and Sibelius's concertos the solo violinist begins almost immediately. When the composer Bengt de Törne told Sibelius years later that he too would be interested in composing a concerto, he received some advice on avoiding the weaknesses of virtuosos: "I warn you especially against long preludes and interludes," Sibelius cautioned. "And this refers particularly to violin concertos. Think of the poor public! What enjoyment can there be in watching a stolid man, and waiting for him to get busy with his Stradivarius or Guarnerius or whatever it be?"[6] Foregoing a lengthy orchestral preamble is one way of defining the relationship between "technical display and musical content."[7] Passages of technical display also have similar structural and harmonic functions in these two concertos. For example, the violinist, Pekka Kuusisto notes that the spiccato string-crossing figurations (measures 440–54) leading to the final virtuosic flourishes of the first movement of the Sibelius violin concerto are reminiscent of the ending of the first movement's cadenza (measures 332–50) in the Mendelssohn violin concerto.[8]

Traces of Beethoven's violin concerto are heard in Sibelius's concerto too. Indeed, violinists such as Rode and Kreutzer, whose works Sibelius studied, were personally known to Beethoven, who was likewise inspired by them when writing his concerto.[9] Kuusisto detects a similarity between the ascending figures of the soloist's entry in

Beethoven's concerto and the ending of the first statement of the second main thematic idea in the first movement of Sibelius's concerto (measures 114–16). Speaking as an interpreter of both these concertos, he conceptualizes the mood at the respective beginnings of their third movements as a bit "rough," as if played with "boots on," rather than "cute" or light-hearted. Thinking further about the musical models for Sibelius, he points out that "it is easy to hear echoes" of Tchaikovsky in a lot of the writing for the soloist in the Sibelius concerto. He draws attention to the influence of Tchaikovsky on Sibelius's First Symphony in E Minor (op. 39) too, and thus takes the listener beyond concerto models.[10] Referring to Sibelius's symphonic conception is apt, not only for his violin concerto but also because his symphonies are viewed, quite often in critical discourses, in terms of Beethoven's and Tchaikovsky's legacies.

While he was working on the Second Symphony in D Major (op. 43) in Rapallo, Italy, in 1901, Sibelius was also outlining the first subject of his concerto's first movement, as his sketch books show. At that time, its melodic idea was already recognizable, and it was labeled "bells in Rapallo."[11] Sibelius revised his ideas about the opening melodic nucleus several times, constructing it in a "painstaking fashion" and changing the initial G-sharp tonality to the final tonic key of D minor.[12] A facsimile of an early version of the autograph score shows that Sibelius originally planned a sustained D-minor chord in the second violin part of the accompaniment, but then changed his mind in favor of moving lines on this chord, as in the first violin part, which avoid a held dissonance between the soloist's sustained G-sharp note (retaining a sense of the initial tonality) and accompanying violins.[13] In addition to the thematic material in his sketchbooks, Sibelius wrote "continuity drafts," which often amounted to whole movements for other works, but which were only fragmentary for the concerto, the longest being just four pages long. It is difficult to determine how the movements developed into their final shapes on the basis of these manuscript drafts, although it seems that the first movement demanded the most attention,[14] as it also did in the revision. Sibelius's correspondence, thematic sketches, and score fragments provide clues, rather than an overall picture, of how musical ideas for the concerto developed. They show that the concerto was planned in parallel with other compositions. Its musical materials are related to those of *Cassazione*; preparatory ideas for the third movement include themes appearing in their final forms in *Music for the Press Celebrations*, the second symphony, and *Kyllikki*; and some drafts from the first movement ended up in *Pohjola's Daughter*.[15]

In the years preceding his work on the concerto, Sibelius undertook intensive study of folk sources, as well as of the techniques of symphonic writing, orchestration, and violin performance. It seemed obvious to early commentators such as Armas Otto Väisänen that Sibelius's compositional thought was influenced by his study of folk sources. Contemporary assessment takes this influence into consideration, particularly since acknowledging it no longer presupposes musicological assumptions about Sibelius as a nationalist composer.[16] Instead, these influences provide a way of thinking about musical geographies, canon formation, and the transnational circulation of musical ideas in the transmission of traditions.

One of Sibelius's influential teachers was the composer Arvid Genetz, who collaborated with Axel August Borenius to collect folk songs in Karelia. Notably, Sibelius met the famous runic singer Larin Paraske in 1891—a meeting that Yrjö Hirn later described: "[Sibelius] was anxious to hear what the Karelian runic melodies were like when they were sung in an authentic way. . . . He listened to her [Paraske] with great attention and made notes on her inflections and rhythm."[17] Sibelius's *Kullervo* was composed following the melodic transcriptions he made of Paraske's performance. Sibelius also consulted Petri Shemeikka, a runic singer in Korpiselkä, eastern Finland, who was recorded singing *Tulen Synty* (The origin of fire) by Armas Launis in 1905.[18] Sibelius regarded Shemeikka as "an ancient spirit so manly and noble," and he claimed that the time he spent with him in the summer of 1892 "was more valuable than any of my best study trips."[19] Listening to these singers led Sibelius to participate in an editorial project to publish a new version of the *Kalevala* with examples of runic melodies (1895) and to deliver an academic paper, in 1896, in which he claimed that an artist steeped in folk music finds artistic fulfillment and develops originality. Sibelius regarded folk music as being only of educational importance for art music, although he pondered the revolutionary potential of its tonalities, and he considered its relation to church modes. He analyzed the oldest Finnish folk songs as being based not on the tonic-dominant relation of Western art tonality but on five notes, D, E, F, G, and A (also the tuning of the five-string kantele, as he noted), which were extended by B-natural and C when the melodic character was intensified. Harmonization in D minor was one option, which lent a somber, chorale-like effect to the melodies.[20] These analytical exercises shaped Sibelius's melodic and harmonic thought.[21] They may have helped Sibelius conceptualize the concerto's opening melody (which he spent much time in crafting and which is the first thematic subject). It is built on the principles of folk tonality that he outlined in his theoretical work, including pitch extensions at moments of melodic intensification. The G-sharp in the violin solo's opening melody falls outside of the basic tonality, presenting an innovative pitch element in the unfolding of the first main subject. The opening melody can be heard in relation to folk tonal stimuli, at least in part. However, it is elaborated immediately with rapid figurations in the solo violin line that depart from any listening based only on the techniques of folk tonality.

A further model relates to Sibelius's synesthetic ability to experience sound and color together. D minor, the tonal center of his violin concerto was the color yellow, according to Karl Ekman, his childhood friend and biographer.[22] Sibelius's ability to see musical sounds drew him closer to the artistic circle living around Lake Tuusula, which he joined in the final stages of composing the concerto. Pekka Halonen had his studio and home there, and the writers Eino Leino and Juhani Aho were also Sibelius's neighbors. Moreover, visual artists also chose violinists as their subjects. Ellen Thesleff painted an unnamed female violinist (*Violin Player*, 1896) using a restricted palette of oil colors to depict "hearing one's inner voice, deep contemplation and the attainment of spirituality."[23] An austerity of color similarly characterized Pekka Halonen's oil paintings *Violinist* (1900) and *Heikki Playing* (1903).[24]

PERFORMERS

Two violinists were linked with the concerto during the compositional process: Wilhelm Burmester and Viktor Nováček, a teacher employed by Wegelius at the Helsinki Music Institute. Sibelius wrote to Aino about the concerto's marvelous themes in 1902, shortly after meeting Burmester, a violinist whom he already knew as a concertmaster in Helsinki in the 1890s, in Berlin. Burmester was one of the leading German violinists of the later nineteenth century and a former student of Joachim at the Hochschule für Ausübende Tonskunst in Berlin (see photograph 3.1). It is

PHOTOGRAPH 3.1 The German violinist Wilhelm Burmester (1869–1933). Photograph by Otto Becker and Maass Berlin. Reproduced with permission from the Sibelius Museum / Stiftelsen för Åbo Akademi, Finland.

possible he asked for the concerto with a plan to premiere the work. Burmester wrote to Sibelius,

> I hardly believe my ears! Is it true what I have been told that you really are working on the long-discussed Violin Concerto and that it will soon be complete? It would be wonderful indeed! Next winter will provide opportunities enough to present it to the public. From you I await something entirely special.[25]

Sibelius responded that he would soon send the violin part with piano reduction and that Burmester would be able to contribute performance indications such as slurs. He flattered Burmester: "I can only dream how it might sound in your masterful hands."[26]

On seeing the first two movements, Burmester wrote to Sibelius in September 1903, "Wonderful! Masterly! Only once before have I spoken in such terms to a composer, and that was when Tchaikovsky showed me his concerto."[27] The following month, on October 5, 1903, a press report in *Hufvudstadsbladet* announced that the concerto was dedicated to Burmester and that he would play the work in March in Finland. Burmester needed more practice time, however, and he wrote to Sibelius at the end of 1903 asking him to delay the premiere.

> Only in recent days have I been able to play through your Concerto with a pianist. . . . I can say to you one thing: "Wonderful!" Rocky nature! I can roughly imagine the effect with the orchestra. It must sound colossal. I am convinced of the future of this Concerto. . . . Our plan to bring the Concerto *ad auris* to the Berliners in February or March must be ceased for good reason. . . . The best option is and will

remain that I play your work in this summer's music festival. There it will be heard and reviewed by the whole press and may at one stroke become popular all over the world.[28]

Sibelius did not wish to delay the premiere. Burmester complained to Sibelius on October 4, 1903, "I have heard from different quarters that you want [Henri] Marteau to play your Violin Concerto in Stockholm and elsewhere. If this is true, I shall *never* play the Concerto. You would make me happy with a couple of lines of explanation." Sibelius responded reassuringly that "the Concerto indeed is dedicated to you and will therefore be played by you alone. . . . I have thought of no-one but you."[29]

Nevertheless, Sibelius insisted on an autumn premiere, and he approached Nováček. But Nováček's performance, which had been announced in the press for January 1904, was postponed too. Nováček complained about the concerto's complexities, especially the "quick passages which he could hardly work out."[30] A month later, Nováček gave the first performance, on February 8, at the University of Helsinki. The program included Sibelius's 1902 cantata, *Tulen Synty* (The origin of fire), *Cassazione*, and *Har du mod?* Tawaststjerna described Nováček as "a mediocrity,"[31] and the premiere, conducted by Sibelius himself, as one in which the "red faced and perspiring" soloist "fought a losing battle with a solo part that bristled with even greater difficulties in this first version than it does in the definitive score."[32] It is a harsh description of the violinist, especially given the limited preparation time available to him.

After its premiere with Nováček as the soloist, Burmester was still in dialogue with Sibelius, assuring the composer:

All my 25 years' platform experience, my artistry and insight will be placed to serve this work. Just this very fact will do much on your work's behalf. Don't worry about anything, just follow your own concerns and leave this safely in my hands. I shall play the concerto in Helsinki in such a way that the city will be at your feet.[33]

Tawaststjerna viewed Sibelius's behavior toward the violinist as "puzzling," but he attributed it to the composer's economic circumstances.[34] In the end, however, Burmester never performed the concerto.

By June 1904, Sibelius had withdrawn the concerto for revision, estimating that he would need another two years to work on it. The intervention of practical and economic factors, however, hastened the revision process. On February 22, 1905, he finalized a new contract with the publisher Robert Lienau, which required him to compose four large-scale works per year. The first year's quota included the revised concerto. Sibelius promised Burmester the premiere of his revision. Yet again there was a scheduling complication. Burmester was not available until autumn 1905, so Lienau suggested that Karel Halíř should be the soloist, with Richard Strauss as conductor of the Berlin Philharmonic. The revised version was premiered in Berlin on October 19, 1905. Strauss conducted from a second set of proofs pasted together.[35]

Sibelius recommended Ysaÿe, Marteau, Kreisler, Kubelik, Petschikoff, and Serato when Lienau asked which virtuosos should be sent a copy. Burmester's name was no longer linked with the work, although Carpelan had recommended sending him the piano score.[36] The revised version was performed in Helsinki on March 12, 1906, with the German violinist Hermann Grevesmühl as soloist and Kajanus conducting the Helsinki Philharmonic. The following month, the Russian violinist Lev Zeitlin performed the concerto in Helsinki. Zeitlin taught violin at the St. Petersburg Conservatory, and by 1932 he was involved with a meritocratic program of music education that would provide training for violinists who were eventually among the most renowned in the world.[37]

The child prodigy Franz von Vécsey also played a prominent role in the early history of the violin concerto (see photograph 3.2). He championed the work after 1910, and he

FRANZ VON VECSEY

PHOTOGRAPH 3.2   The Hungarian violinist Franz von Vécsey. Photograph by Ernst Schneider. Reproduced with permission from the Sibelius Museum / Stiftelsen för Åbo Akademi, Finland.

became the dedicatee of Sibelius's revised version.[38] Vécsey began studies with his father and continued from the age of eight with the Hungarian violinist Jenö Hubay.[39] Carl Flesch described Hubay's students as having a developed left-hand technique and a "natural feeling for tonal beauty."[40] Hubay dedicated his own third concerto to Vécsey, and he performed Bach's double violin concerto with him in London in 1908. Vécsey also studied with Joachim, who thought of him as the greatest living violinist and recommended him to his former student Auer. In 1905, Vécsey performed in St. Petersburg. Auer was eager to hear him, later writing that he was "deeply impressed by an execution well-nigh perfect from a technical point of view, but one which was coupled with tonal pallor and lack of temperament, though real musical feeling was apparent in all that he played."[41]

Vécsey performed Sibelius's violin concerto in 1909 in Berlin,[42] when Sibelius was also working in the city. Following this performance, Sibelius commented in a diary entry, "A fine musician. But the Concerto itself will still have to wait. Scorn will be poured on it. Or what is worse, a passing condescending mention."[43] In 1914, Sibelius spent another month working in Berlin, composing a commissioned work and attending concerts. In his diary, he reported that he went to visit Vécsey, who "played in the new style"—which left Sibelius wondering, "What will become of this man?"[44] (In fact, Vécsey served in the Austro-Hungarian armed forces during World War I, though he returned to the concert stage in the 1920s.)[45]

Many of the performers associated in one way or another with this work, including Burmester, Nováček, Halíř, and Vécsey, had once been Joachim's students, as had Sibelius's own violin teacher in Berlin, Fritz Strauss.[46] Joachim's opinion of the 1905 revision should have mattered. He advised his students to ignore the concerto. He thought it was "awful and tedious," a view Sibelius dismissed by responding that Joachim "no longer seems to understand the emotional life of the time."[47] Yet Joachim was not alone in his critical view; the concerto was "ahead of its time, and only the following generation acknowledged its worth," Lienau noted in his memoires.[48]

CRITICS

Critics offered mixed opinions on the concerto. Some commentators on the 1904 premiere had been critical of the work's structural features and the demands it placed on the soloist. But they also showed signs of enthusiasm. Karl Flodin was an important critical voice, and he assessed the work at length:

> It is quite clear that the composer did not want to write the sort of violin concerto that is nothing else than a symphonic work with an *obligato* solo violin. He well knew the fate of these modern concertos; once played and then discarded. Under these circumstances he preferred the other alternative: to let the soloist be the sovereign master the whole time and incidentally develop all the traditional pomp and circumstance. But in so doing he ran into the compact mass of everything that has been said, written and composed before him. It was impossible to invent anything really new! And the vessel stranded on these hidden rocks.[49]

Flodin, as one of Sibelius's former teachers, also wrote with much advice. He suggested that Sibelius had yielded to conventional virtuoso writing and that with some changes the concerto could be a significant work. Flodin pointed out the "overflow of musical ideas and technical difficulties," and he complained about a lack of memorable melodic ideas such as those found in the violin concertos of Beethoven, Mendelssohn, Bruch, Brahms, and Tchaikovsky.[50]

The composer and critic Oskar Merikanto offered a more favorable assessment. Sibelius's concerto "met great expectations," though for a successful performance the third movement needed a "Burmester technique."[51] Merikanto himself had dedicated at least one of his own compositions to Burmester. He also wrote that the "role of the orchestra is, by the way, rather strange and exceptional," and he praised Nováček's "masterly performance of the difficult task"; in fact, the Adagio, as performed by Nováček, had to be repeated due to audience demand. The critic Alarik Uggla predicted that the concerto would become a "cherished repertoire number for outstanding violin virtuosos," and Evert Katila suggested that some revisions would ensure the concerto a "worthy position in the new violin repertoire."[52]

A performance in 1914 in Berlin (possibly with Vécsey as soloist) prompted harsh reviews, which affected Sibelius greatly. He commented, "To be treated with such contempt at my age is wounding. I must reconcile myself to being out of the game but nevertheless go my own way forward."[53] After a 1928 performance in Berlin, Heinrich Strobel wrote that the concerto was an "insipid piece, creeping along in shapeless monotony," and that there was no "genuine violin virtuosity," while Alfred Einstein commented that it was not clear if the first movement aimed at being "concertante or symphonic."[54]

Critics in the United States were both appreciative and appalled when Maud Powell premiered the work in 1906 at Carnegie Hall, a performance that foreshadowed the work's significance in developing the careers of female virtuosos. A *New York Times* critic wrote of its "paucity of ideas"; a writer for the *New York Sun* wondered why Powell put her "magnificent art into this sour and crabbed concerto"; and the critic for the *New York Evening Post* predicted that the concerto's "rugged Northern character, its lack of sensuous beauty and smoothness—though there are lovely, calm moments—will stand in its way."[55] The critic H. E. Krehbiel recalled in the *New York Tribune* that Powell had introduced Tchaikovsky's Violin Concerto in D Major (op. 35) to American audiences. He continued: "It is now Mr. Sibelius's turn. The Finnish composer has put out his dragnet and captured a multitude of curiosities in the way of difficulties never seen before. . . . All the heights of the violin are furiously scaled in this new concerto, and all its most lugubrious depths explored."[56] Similarly, William B. Chase wrote a review for the *New York Evening Sun*:

It was a new departure in solo repertory. Forbidding in its true Finnish darkness of outlook, the music was rhapsodic and epic by turns, the solo persistently set off against a Greek chorus of cellos, a background of mysterious deep horns or an uplifting choir of wood voices. Here is one of the few concertos that speak.[57]

All of the American critics recognized Powell's virtuosity. She also performed Samuel Coleridge-Taylor's Violin Concerto in G Minor (op. 80) in 1912 and was its dedicatee.[58] Sibelius sent a message to her before the American premiere of his work: "To the Violin Queen, Miss Maud Powell, with gratitude."[59] Unfortunately, there is no recording of Powell's performance of the Sibelius violin concerto, but there is one of her playing his *Valse Triste* (⊙ see audio-visual example 3.1 on the website).[60]

Successors continued to perform Sibelius's concerto in the United States. Olin Downes wrote to Sibelius on December 30, 1930, noting that Efrem Zimbalist had presented it in such a way that the public might realize "what an extremely interesting and effective work this concerto could be under circumstances of an adequate performance."[61]

In Britain, Cecil Gray was impressed by the concerto's balance between "brilliant and effective" virtuosity and musical interest, especially its original structural form (such as the cadenza that precedes the development section in the first movement). He described the second movement as a "gradual unfolding, like a flower, of a long, sweet, *cantabile* melody first presented by the solo instrument and then by the orchestra."[62] Despite his comment that thinking about musical nationality was "wearisome," Gray detected a "national flavour" based on resemblances with folk song in the B-flat minor episode of the first movement and the second subject of the third.[63] Donald Francis Tovey wrote that the concerto was original, masterly and exhilarating, and that it had "huge and simple" outlines.[64] On the other hand, no less a champion of the composer than Robert Layton was critical, years later, of the "superbly written" work, attributing its popularity to the fact that "violinists love playing it" even though it was not Sibelius "at his best."[65] He was particularly critical of the work's thematic development, seeing a lack thereof and regarding this as its crucial weakness. This lack is made all too clear to listeners, according to Layton, because the opening theme is "heaven-sent"; it is "so superior in quality to the material that succeeds it that it seems a difference almost in kind rather than degree."[66] He failed to recognize either the interweaving of the opening theme into the orchestral texture or the cadenza as a development of it, describing the latter only as having the virtuosic qualities of Vieuxtemps.[67] Layton considered the second movement "considerably weaker" with a self-indulgent "lushness," and he questioned the addition of trumpets in the orchestration of the second thematic idea.[68] By contrast, he described the third movement as the "most brilliant and exciting" and the rhythmic interplay between 6/8 and 3/4 as "effective," with a sense of momentum that "even in an inferior performance never fails to rivet the attention of an audience."[69] He was more enthusiastic about other music that Sibelius wrote for the violin, which he considered as displaying "unforced charm and spontaneity," "lightness of touch," and "freshness of sparkle."[70]

THE REVISED CONCERTO

The violin concerto is in three movements. The first movement (Allegro moderato in D minor) begins with the statement of the first thematic subject (see music example 3.1), which continuously folds over its tonal center of D but culminates with a surprising E-flat before plunging to the violin's lowest register. It has an exploratory quality, supported only by the violins with a dynamic marking of pianissimo, until the string texture is momentarily interrupted when a solo clarinet echoes the soloist's opening

Measures 1–8 of the first movement of Sibelius's violin concerto.

figure of a descending fifth (measures 11–14). This echo immediately alerts the listener to the melodic importance of the soloist's opening three notes.

The musical texture is built on the soloist's contrasting registers in the thematic elaboration from measure 33 onward. Over a timpani drone (a blurred tonal center of D because of a continuous trill effect), the soloist crosses the violin's registers with ascending figurations while the bassoon plays lines in the low pitch range and four horns make an entry with sustained chords. A short non-thematic cadenza passage follows at the end of measure 53, which begins by rapidly ascending the G string to emphasize the violin's deepest sonorities. This passage precedes a lyrical one in which melodic themes are first stated by the bassoons and cellos, and a countermelody is played pizzicato by the double basses in divided octaves. The clarinets introduce the second main thematic melody (in measure 97), which is marked *molto moderato e tranquillo*. It is repeated in D-flat major with the soloist initially playing double stops, mainly sixths and octaves (see music example 3.2) and then a single line in dialogue with a solo viola's countermelody (measures 106–13). The soloist breathes. Sibelius literally wrote breathing into the soloist's part, with semiquaver and quaver rests in the violin's melodic line, as if for a singer, in a section with the performance directions *largamente* (broadly), *espressivo* (expressively), and *affettuoso* (tenderness).

A second orchestral episode (measures 127–221) introduces and develops an energetic melodic idea in the violin sections, which is supported by sustained harmonic textures in the woodwinds, horns, and lower strings. The orchestral texture becomes more subdued in the lead-up to the soloist's cadenza, which is structurally placed in the development section rather than as a final flourish at the end of the movement. The soloist further develops the first main theme, which is also stated by the bassoons toward the end of the cadenza (measures 271–80). The recapitulation section continues to develop the thematic ideas, and fortissimo descending lines in the horns, trumpets, trombones, and timpani (measures 351–57) intensify the lush orchestral textures to usher in the soloist's restatement of the second

MUSIC EXAMPLE 3.2   Measures 101–3 of the first movement of Sibelius's violin concerto.

main theme (arriving fully in measure 372). The first movement ends with a final virtuosic flourish of octaves, string crossings, and scale passages.

The second movement (Adagio di molto) in B-flat major is an exemplary treatment of cooperation between the soloist and the orchestra; in fact, it is a duet throughout, a compelling vision of the ideal balance between soloist and orchestra. Structurally, too, it is as if the orchestra holds up a mirror for the soloist in the second part, so that the beauty of the solo violin's opening melodic line can be both shared with and reflected back to the soloist. The movement begins with the interplay of the woodwinds, in which the clarinets hand the melody over to the oboes. The woodwind texture is augmented momentarily by the flutes before the melodic lines retreat back to the clarinets descending in thirds. The entry of four horns and two bassoons provides the textural backdrop for the soloist's presentation of one of Sibelius's most intense, lyrical, and meditative melodies, played on the violin's lowest string to achieve maximum sonorous depth. The violin's descending interval of a diminished fifth (from B-flat to E-natural), in bar 9, is punctuated by the dissonance of a rising B-flat broken chord in the double basses (see music example 3.3), and the E-natural contrasts with both the preceding and subsequent accented

MUSIC EXAMPLE 3.3   Measures 6–13 of the second movement of Sibelius's violin concerto.

E-flats in the melodic line. Rhythmic momentum is gained by moving into triplet figurations.

The solo melodic line develops in intensity as the strings are added to the instrumental texture. Its descending and ascending arcs are reiterated in a section of contrapuntal writing for the soloist, who plays in double stops over a static harmonic texture in the strings and horns (see music example 3.4).

From measure 42 onward, the orchestra takes over the main melodic material even as the soloist continues to be a prominent voice in the musical texture, playing accented rising lines, trills, and a descending line that diminishes in volume and leads to pianissimo broken octaves. This movement ends with the performance direction *morendo* (dying out), and it dissipates into silence.

The third movement begins with a rhythmically vigorous thematic idea in the violin solo line, which is often perceived

MUSIC EXAMPLE 3.4   Measures 32–34 of the second movement of Sibelius's violin concerto.

JEAN SIBELIUS'S VIOLIN CONCERTO

Measures 5–8 of the third movement of Sibelius's violin concerto (solo violin part).

Measures 72–75 of the third movement of Sibelius's violin concerto (solo violin part).

as having a dance-like character (see music example 3.5). It is repeated two octaves higher before launching into scale-type runs, arpeggios, staccato thirds, and an ascending passage based on the elaboration of a diminished chord. The orchestral accompaniment is rhythmically consistent, and an emerging continuous semiquaver pattern is almost drone-like in its effect.

A second theme, playful in character, is presented first by the orchestra and then by the soloist (from measure 64 onward). It is elaborated through double-stopping, and it plays on a rhythmic contrast between off- and on-beat entries, the latter emphasized by three-note chords for a fuller texture, as well as louder dynamic indications (see music example 3.6).

These two themes form the basis for the third movement. Sibelius gives the final flourish to the soloist, accompanied by the orchestra. The final eight bars feature rapid scalar runs and an arpeggio ascent marked *cresc. possible* (increasing the volume as much as possible) to the final accented D in the solo violinist's top range.

The 1905 revision focused on the soloist's role. In particular, Sibelius cut out a cadenza, described as "Bach-like," which might have been in the original because of the initial plan that Burmester, who was praised by contemporaries for his interpretations of Bach, would premiere the work.[71] Appropriately, Sibelius's own emotional investment in violin performance led to a work that stretched the virtuoso in technical and interpretative terms, but ultimately he revised it from the perspective of compositional self-reflection. He contemplated writing a second concerto, though he used its sketch material in the Sixth Symphony in D Minor (op. 104) instead.[72]

After the 1905 performance, Lienau informed Sibelius that Strauss viewed the work as "poorly orchestrated."[73] In 1930, Lienau asked Sibelius if he could make changes to the orchestration and add metronome markings, because conductors had reported some of the rhythms were difficult for musicians, particularly in the last movement. Sibelius did not add metronome markings, at least not immediately. He wanted performers to have some freedom with respect to tempi choices. However, the tempo marking for the third movement now in the score was based on Anja Ignatius's interpretation, as one of her former students, the conductor Jukka-Pekka Saraste, noted. Sibelius became somewhat frustrated that performances of the third movement were sometimes too fast, and he asked Ignatius about her tempo, which he considered to be perfectly in accordance with the performance marking *allegro, ma non tanto*.[74]

Sibelius did not change the brass and woodwind writing that conductors commented on, though he considered the possibility. Eventually, performers met the work's technical demands, and orchestral balance improved, so Lienau's request became irrelevant.[75] Sibelius had been attentive to orchestration throughout his career, especially to its symbolic dimensions. He studied orchestration in Vienna and purchased François-Auguste Gevaert's 1885 treatise on instrumentation, *Neue Instrumenten-Lehre*, informing Wegelius of his acquisition. Sibelius paid particular attention to woodwinds and percussion, and he asked instrumentalists to offer him practical advice as he worked on *Kullervo*.[76] Later, Sibelius advised the following with respect to writing for these sections of the orchestra:

> You must never write anything without knowing exactly how it will sound. By employing unusual registers of instruments you can sometimes obtain quite new and interesting colours. But this does not mean that you should go in for extravagant experiments. . . . Let us take an instance. Suppose you wish to write a third and let the lowest tone of the flute play its fundamental note: you can very well give the upper note to the tuba. But, whereas the flute has a very striking colour, the top register of the tuba is completely devoid of any trace of character and just sounds like a bad and weak horn. So the only result will be that your invention looks "interesting" in the score.[77]

Sibelius's caution to distinguish between how notes are written on the page and how they sound stems from a deep appreciation for the performer. In fact, the relation between a score and its realization in performance has prompted a debate about the division of labor and musical hierarchies between composer and performer. In this debate, the composer is often seen as creative. The virtuoso, who studies a score in depth, pondering and memorizing every detail, is often seen as only realizing the composer's intentions. Thus, virtuosity seems to be the "accomplishment of the impossible" with the effect of "magic," but since it demands a profound engagement with the score, it actually marks "servitude," because the performer is "wired to notational prescriptions."[78]

Is the audience a witness to spectacles of servitude or of magic? There are elements of both in virtuosity, which help to overturn old models about the division of labor. Pedagogues like Auer, Ivan Galamian, and Dorothy DeLay have emphasized that the close study of a score should lead to individual musical interpretations. This means that in the hands of performers there are multiple versions of the Sibelius violin concerto, because each player approaches the work creatively and afresh. Musical scores can be viewed in more general terms, too, as derived from faculties of thought and as material symbols of a human capacity for communication. Thus, Virno's claim that we are all virtuosos because we speak is a broad view of human communication,[79] and it is close to Auer's understanding of violin virtuoso performance as a declamation.[80] It takes us away from the specific compositional circumstances of Sibelius's concerto to the place of this work in the longer traditions of violin playing.

CHAPTER 4

REGIONAL AND TRANSNATIONAL TRADITIONS OF VIOLIN PLAYING

S IBELIUS'S MUSICAL IDEAS AND performers' interpretations of his violin concerto are shaped by different
violin-playing traditions. Indeed, instrumental techniques
and musical aesthetics have been shaped across art and folk
genres throughout violin-playing history. When the violin
first made its way over the Alps to France around 1535, it
was viewed as an instrument fit only "for fiddling in taverns
and at the country dances of the peasantry.[1] Jean-Baptiste
Lully, having begun his musical career as a street performer
in Italy, changed this view of the violin when he ended up in
the employment of Louis XIV of France. Lully introduced
greater ensemble discipline within his orchestra, and he
raised the violin's status by the mid-seventeenth century to
that of the "king of orchestral instruments."[2]

Jean Sibelius's Violin Concerto. Tina K. Ramnarine, Oxford University Press (2020). © Oxford University Press.
DOI: 10.1093/oso/9780190611538.001.0001

The violin was introduced to the Swedish court during the reign of Queen Kristina (from 1632 to 1654). She employed musicians from France from 1646 onward. By 1682, the violin had become a popular instrument across Sweden, and employment opportunities for French and also German musicians had extended to the courts of other Swedish nobles. Known as a "violin" in the circles of the Swedish nobility, the instrument in its more crudely constructed version was called a "fiol" or "fela" (fiddle).[3] The violin spread through Finland via Sweden during the eighteenth and nineteenth centuries. It became a popular folk instrument with a repertoire of wedding marches, polskas, and minuets. By the end of the nineteenth century, violins and fiddles had become important instruments in urban popular music across this region, as well as throughout Europe.

In composing the violin concerto, Sibelius benefited from familiarity with the Franco-Belgian and Russian schools of violin playing, as well as with regional folk violin-playing traditions. He began his studies with nineteenth-century violin playing models and he lived to witness mid twentieth-century developments, including the growth of conservatory-trained violinists and the revival of folk-playing traditions on a national scale.[4] Like any work of its kind, Sibelius's violin concerto is located historically in the spread of the violin and the development over time of a range of violin-playing traditions.

Folk dance repertoires inflect discourses on Sibelius's violin concerto, mainly with regard to its third movement. The musicologist Erkki Salmenhaara referred to the movement's "restless, demonic character" and to an "inner, forward-moving energy" created by the first subject's dotted rhythms.[5] The violinist Ida Haendel described it as a "danse macabre," referring to Tovey's comment that it is "a polonaise for polar bears" (⏵ see audio-visual example 4.1 on the website).[6]

In representations of musical exoticism, Tovey further commented that it is a finale that "achieves gigantic proportions and brilliant high spirits" and leads the listener "to Finland, or to whatever Fairyland Sibelius will have us attain" through dance.[7] Another musicologist, Tomi Mäkelä, considered the polonaise a nineteenth-century topos, a basic literary motif, which featured in a number of works that might have provided Sibelius with musical models. Sibelius possessed a score of Spohr's Twelfth Violin Concerto in A Major, op. 79 (1828). The final movement of this concerto is labeled *Alla polacca* ("in the Polish style"), which, like Karl Goldmark's Concerto in A Minor, op. 28 (1878), resembles the rhythmic arrangement of Sibelius's concerto.[8] The topos of the polonaise seemed relevant to debates on musical nationalism, since it evoked ideas about self-government with reference to Poland's political circumstances as a part of the Russian Empire. The elaboration of traditional dance music in new artworks was partly related to defining musical nationalism, but a more important point was the "future of the genre," namely, the concerto's continued relevance as a vehicle for demonstrating musical virtuosity.[9]

Sibelius maintained a lifelong interest in folk repertoires. He heard Einojuhani Rautavaara's folk-based composition *Pelimannit* (The folk musicians, 1952) on the radio and recommended him for a scholarship from the music foundation of the conductor Sergei Koussevitzky. It was awarded in honor of Sibelius's ninetieth birthday. Rautavaara's composition drew on material from an ethnographic source, Ilmari Krohn's compilation *Vanhoja Pelimannisävelmiä* (Old folk compositions, 1893–97), which was later republished by the Finnish Literature Society in 1975.[10] With Rautavaara, as with Sibelius himself, folk violin practice is a musical resource that informs art compositions and vice versa.[11]

Sibelius's interests probably extended to the links between art and folk violin techniques in Russian as well as Finnish contexts. St. Petersburg was nearby, and he had received training from a Russian violin teacher, which connected him with the more widespread use of ethnographic collections in national art forms. In Russia, the links between art and folk practices were strong. The early formation of the Russian violin school had been shaped in equal part by folk and baroque playing techniques. Private musical events had become integral to Russian aristocratic social life by the mid-eighteenth century. So too had the employment of musicians from central Europe for teaching posts in Russia. Italian violinists were favored, some of whom served in Russian courts for decades. The Italian baroque playing techniques they introduced, including the composition of improvisatory pieces, cadenzas, and études showcasing highly developed technical skills, combined with the Russian folk performing styles of local musicians, many of whom were from serf backgrounds. Art forms gained social prestige, and the status of soloists rose. Catherine the Great supported solo violinists playing Russian folk-like pieces in a politically informed system of patronage aimed at "cultivating Russian art and fostering highly-skilled Russian musicians."[12] The concert-master of Catherine's court orchestra, Ivan Yefstafyevich Khandoshkin, spent some years studying in Italy, especially with Giuseppe Tartini, and he gained widespread recognition throughout Europe. He extended violin techniques in his own compositions (violin sonatas) by combining Italian styles (especially Tartini's bowing techniques, as set out in *The Art of Bowing: Variations on a Theme by Corelli*, 1758) with Russian folk performing traditions. Techniques from the Russian folk tradition included improvising on both the violin and balalaika and making use of three- and four-note chords and tenths, as well as spiccato bowing, trills, and left-hand pizzicato combined with right-hand bowed passages to imitate balalaika techniques. Khandoshkin was an influential teacher with appointments at the Imperial Academy of the Arts and the Knipper Theatre. His students continued to improvise with Russian folk repertoires and performance techniques. For example, Ivan Fedorovich Yablochkin continued his teacher's practices of collecting folk materials for composing violin solos in a Russian style. These techniques of performance and composition provided the foundations of the twentieth-century Russian violin school.[13] This constituted another potential model for Sibelius as he explored folk traditions.

The Hungarian violinist and pedagogue Leopold Auer embodied an important and direct connection between Sibelius and the Russian violin school. He became a central figure in the St. Petersburg Conservatory, and his students came to define the Russian school. His influence on the spread of Sibelius's concerto is significant, not least because his students championed the work.

It is likely that Sibelius heard Auer perform Mendelssohn's violin concerto in Finland during his years as a student at the Helsinki Music Institute. Auer had moved to St. Petersburg to take up a conservatory post at the invitation of Anton Rubinstein. Ysaÿe and Taneiev played Sibelius's violin concerto for Auer in St. Petersburg when Sibelius visited him there. The newspaper *Helsingin Sanomat* dedicated its music column of June 7, 1945, to celebrating the centenary of Auer's birth, noting that he had been influential for Finnish violinists and that he had last visited Finland in 1917.[14] Franz von Vécsey, the dedicatee of Sibelius's concerto, also studied with Auer.

In his autobiography, *My Long Life in Music*, Auer wrote about different violin schools in relation to national geographies of learning. He outlined the dominance of the Italian school in the eighteenth century and of the French and Belgian schools in the nineteenth. He mentioned the major figures of these schools, including, from the Franco-Belgian tradition, Kreutzer, Rode, Vieuxtemps, and Bériot,[15] whose repertoire Sibelius had also studied as a violinist. Auer himself trained in the Franco-Belgian school (⊙ see audio-visual example 4.2 on the website).[16] At the St. Petersburg Conservatory, he trained some of the most celebrated violinists of the twentieth century, such as Mischa Elman, Efrem Zimbalist, Jascha Heifetz, David Oistrakh, Toscha Seidel, and Michel Piastro. His assistant was Ovanes Arakelovich Nalbandian, who also taught nearly all of Auer's outstanding students.[17]

Auer did not endorse strict notions of tradition, preferring to stress individuality, but he did recognize the transmission of playing styles through musical lineages. His own musical lineage was a distinguished one. He studied the violin with the concertmaster of the National Opera, Ridley Kohné, at the Budapest Conservatory, who organized his debut as soloist in Mendelssohn's concerto at a benefit concert given by the National Opera. This concert was followed by further study with Jacob Dont in Vienna. Two years later, Auer was traveling as a child prodigy, aged thirteen, giving concerts to support his family in Hungary. He played for Karl Goldmark and later on for Vieuxtemps, whose wife accompanied Auer but complained about his over-sentimental glissandi, which she described as sounding like a cat "miaowing in every key."[18] In 1861, Auer studied with Jean-Delphin Alard at the Paris Conservatoire and then for two years with Joseph Joachim in Hanover. When Auer was short of funds, he would play Spohr's duos and Bach's double violin concerto with his teacher at the private concerts of King George V.[19] He considered Joachim an inspiration, from whom he learned to work with his head as well as his hands.[20] Joachim was a priestlike figure for Auer, "thrilling his congregation with a sermon revealing the noblest moral beauties of a theme which could not help but interest all humanity" and teaching by example rather than explanation.[21] Joachim composed a violin concerto, the *Hungarian* Concerto, which his students included in their repertoire. Although it was not widely played, Tovey described it as "one of the most important documents of the middle of the nineteenth century"[22] because it allowed Joachim to develop "the full resources of his instrument" and the experience he needed to assist the composer Johannes Brahms.[23] At the age of nineteen, Auer became the concertmaster of the orchestra of the concert society of Düsseldorf, and during the early stages of his career he met Brahms and the composers Hector Berlioz and Gioachino Rossini (▶ see audio-visual examples 4.3 and 4.4, in English, as well as audio-visual examples 4.5 and 4.6, in the original Russian, on the website).[24]

In his book *Violin Playing as I Teach It*, Auer mentioned Burmester,[25] another Joachim student, who he esteemed highly as displaying intrinsic musicianship. Contemporary listeners can gain an impression of Burmester's musicianship through old recordings that have been posted online (▶ see audio-visual example 4.7 on the website).[26] Auer's assessment is worth noticing, given not only the drama over the premiere of Sibelius's violin concerto but also Burmester's difficulties with Piotr Ilich Tchaikovsky. Correspondence indicates that Burmester played Tchaikovsky's concerto for the composer in 1888. He hoped he would perform it with Tchaikovsky conducting in Helsinki, according to a letter written in 1893, though the latter's schedule did not permit it. In the end, Tchaikovsky seems to have tired of the young violinist seeking performance opportunities and letters of recommendation.[27] Burmester's relation with Tchaikovsky ended unhappily, as it did with Sibelius.

In 1872, Auer succeeded Henri Wieniawski at the St. Petersburg Conservatory and held the post of "Soloist to His Majesty the Emperor," which entailed playing solos for ballets. When he retired from this role he maintained the title of "Soloist to the Czar."[28] He gained unique insights into musical life in the Russian court, describing the work of the Imperial Ballet School (from which the membership of Sergei Diaghilev's *Ballets Russes* would be constituted later on) and the musical dinner parties of Grand Duke Constantine (the brother of Alexander II), who became president of the Imperial Russian Society of Music in 1871. The grand duke was a patron of the artistic movement to develop a national Russian musical culture, and he supported a library of scores by Mikhail Glinka and Alexander Serov. Every Friday afternoon, musicians from the Imperial Opera Orchestra would join the grand duke, who played the cello, to play through works that had been arranged for organ and string quintet.[29] Under his patronage, the conservatory became an imperial institution, and students completing diploma studies enjoyed civic rights throughout the Russian Empire.

Auer highlighted these civic rights as a noteworthy privilege in a class-stratified society. He provided an account of the economic arrangements underpinning musical life:

> Only a few years after Alexander II had abolished serfdom, the custom of classifying a man according to birth, or according to his functions in the state hierarchy, was so deeply rooted that the desire to belong to one of the privileged classes—there were thirteen of them—seemed altogether natural. In addition, there was the question of financial advantage. All government functionaries and officials were exempt from direct taxation by the state, unless they owned lands, city residences, or coupon-bearing investments. And even these had been taxed only since the end of the Russo-Turkish War of 1877. Hence, thanks to the measure which placed the musical membership of the Conservatoires under the protection of the Imperial eagle, all the professors and the directors were unquestionably ranged in one of the social classes privileged to advance.[30]

These civic rights bring klezmer into view as another violin-playing tradition that is part of the broader cultural context and history of Sibelius's violin concerto. Civic rights gave Jewish students at conservatories access to St. Petersburg and Moscow, cities that were otherwise largely closed to them due to legal restrictions on their free movement. Jewish students were not allowed to make up more than 5 percent of the total student body in those cities, a ruling from which the St. Petersburg Conservatory was exempt due to the initiatives of its director (the cellist Karl Davidoff) and president (the grand duke). However, students could not be accompanied by their parents. Alexander Glazunov, Auer's last director, intervened in the case of Heifetz, who was "admitted to the Conservatoire without question in view of his talent,"[31] and Auer also accepted Jascha's father as a student.

Jewish violinists shaped performance styles at the conservatory. The ethnomusicologist Mark Slobin noted that Auer was "most responsible for shifting Russian klezmer energy into classical channels," and he credited the violin pedagogue with recognizing the complexities of an ornament like the *krekhts* (stopping the string and flicking the finger), which combined "the technical, the aesthetic, and the national."[32] Auer taught many violinists from families of klezmorim, including Elman and David Oistrakh, and the "Russian sound" has been described as incorporating klezmer violin techniques such as a lot of vibrato and portamento into more traditionally classical modes of playing.[33] Heifetz moved to St. Petersburg from Vilnius, a city that was itself a focal point for Jewish communities in the northwest region of the Russian Empire. The scholar Mosei Beregovsky noted that klezmer musicians sought employment in ensembles in Vilnius; they provided entertainment for parks and restaurants during the early twentieth century.[34] Later in the twentieth century, violinists from this klezmer background who trained with Auer would have a profound impact on violin playing worldwide. Among them, the violinists Oistrakh and Heifetz would become well-known performers of Sibelius's violin concerto. The Finnish violinist Anja Ignatius appreciated Oistrakh's interpretation of the concerto, and she commented favorably on his rendition of the opening melody (⊙ see audio-visual example 4.8 on the website).[35,36]

The place of these violinists in the story of Sibelius's violin concerto means that this work stands at the crossroads of different nationalisms. During his years of study, Heifetz collaborated with members of the Society for Jewish Folk Music, which was founded in St. Petersburg in 1908 by conservatory students and cultural activists. The society's aim to develop Jewish music was informed by the ethnographic collections of Jewish folk songs that were published by the Jewish Historical-Ethnographic Society. Musical arrangements and compositions based on folk materials contributed to the idea of developing Jewish national art music.[37] Composers incorporated melodies from Torah cantillation, prayer chant, Hasidic *nigunim*, wedding dances played by klezmer ensembles, and songs from Yiddish theatre. They also "added harmonic accompaniment and virtuosic passages for the violin, expanded musical forms, and made other significant alterations in adapting music that originated in the synagogue and the home for the classical concert hall."[38] Heifetz performed and recorded many of these compositions. He edited pieces like Joseph Achrom's *Hebrew Melody* in 1933, and he arranged ethnographically-influenced virtuoso display pieces, including works based on the music of Roma bands, such as *Hora Staccato* (1932).[39] In programming these kinds of short recital pieces, Heifetz was influenced by the Austrian violinist Fritz Kreisler, who composed "baroque miniatures."[40] Across Europe, composers turned to folk playing traditions as a way of forging distinctive musical and political identities, which were based on ideas about national and rural cultural capacities. Ethnographic collections and recordings influenced the composition of "rural miniatures" (as Walden calls them),[41] such as Manuel de Falla's *Siete canciones populares españolas* and Béla Bartók's *Romanian Folk Dances*. Loeffler suggests that the legacy of the Society for Jewish Folk Music on Jewish cultural life in Russia, the United States, and elsewhere has been significant. This is certainly true in tracing the legacies of both Heifetz and Auer in violin histories.

Auer wrote his autobiography as a witness to the political circumstances of his time. It is a record of pedagogic processes in the formation of a violin performance tradition in which he played an important role. Auer left Russia in 1917 for a concert tour, traveling across Finland to Tornio, which was at the time on Russia's frontier. Tornio, he observed, had become a place of "the greatest importance," for its river—on the other side of which lay Sweden—was the site of heavy traffic.[42] Crossing this border, Auer gave some concerts in Norway. On his return journey in October, he met a friend from St. Petersburg in Stockholm, who advised him to delay his travel, as it seemed likely that the Bolsheviks would overthrow the Russian Provisional Government. The Revolution meant that Auer never returned to St. Petersburg. A lengthy career in that city cut short by political circumstances gave rise to his autobiographical insights into Russian musical life. His signed photographs from this period (see photograph 4.1) reveal that he met violinists in Finland, including Ruth Ringbom, to whom Sibelius had dedicated an early violin piece, the Andante Cantabile in G Major composed in 1887.

When Auer moved to the United States he taught at the Julliard School of Music and at the Curtis Institute, thus contributing to a violin-playing tradition stretching

PHOTOGRAPH 4.1   A signed photograph of the Hungarian violinist Leopold Auer (1845–1930), which was presented to the violinist Ruth Ringbom (the aunt of the Sibelius biographer Nils-Eric Ringbom) on January 19, 1917. Reproduced with permission from the Sibelius Museum / Stiftelsen för Åbo Akademi, Finland.

across the Atlantic. His autobiography concludes with his impressions of America's musical life, as well as comments on the potential for general music education to foster a new generation of performers. His publications and his teaching practice in the United States were part of a tradition of European pedagogic influence on American violinists, which included the circulation and citation of ideas from method books by Spohr, Francesco Geminiani, and others.[43] Ivan Galamian was one of Auer's teaching assistants in the United States. Later on, Dorothy DeLay became Galamian's assistant and eventually established her own violin class at Juilliard, with students such as Itzhak Perlman and Sarah Chang.

Auer's assertion that the repertoire of one's own era helps performers to develop technical and interpretative skills applies to Sibelius's violin concerto. Following its premiere, it has extended violin virtuosity to the present day. Many violinists traveled to perform in Finland in the years following the premiere, including Carl Flesch, Mischa Elman, Kathleen Parlow, Carlotta Stubenrauch, Alexander Mogilewsky, Alessandro Cortani, and Jacques Thibaud. This list highlights three significant features of violin performing traditions in the early twentieth century: a transnational network, the strong concert presence of violinists trained in the St. Petersburg Conservatory, and the emergence of women soloists.[44] Auer's influence on violin-playing styles was central in all these respects.

In *Violin Playing as I Teach It*, Auer devoted a chapter to style. He urged violinists to develop an individual temperament and to be aware of the changing aesthetics from one era to another. The violinist should contemplate stylistic issues not in terms of historical development but in terms of beauty and truth, as they are conceptualized in one's own time. He wrote that "respect for tradition" requires caution, since it "weighs down the living spirit of the present with the dead formalism of the past."[45] For Auer, style is a "temporary crystallization, at various periods, of the ideals of violin interpretation best suited to the intellectual and musical feeling of the periods in questions, *and born of the violin music of those periods itself*."[46] Moreover, style, Auer explained, is influenced by the material qualities of the instrument:

> The high model violins, such as those of the Stainer type, speak more readily, while the flatter violins of the Cremona school have more carrying power and flexibility, and their tone is more susceptible to subtle variations by the player. That the greater interpretative possibilities of the Cremona type have had their favourable influence on violin composition is more than probable.[47]

A technically proficient violinist, one who is capable of making the violin speak and sing in Auer's theory of vocality, might be able to persuade an audience "with compelling power . . . like all other artists whose appeal is addressed to the multitude."[48] Auer and Flesch presented this theory, according to which the violin speaks and gives expression to a player's inner voice, in treatises.[49] The capacity to speak through the violin[50] depended on an integrated technique according to the violinist Raphael Bronstein. For him, the bow is like a painter's brush, but an "ineffectual" one if there is no clear articulation in a left hand that "speaks."[51] Bronstein was one of Auer's teaching assistants in the United

States (and a former student in St. Petersburg). His method book, *The Science of Violin Playing*, includes a performance analysis of Sibelius's violin concerto, in which he imagined the concerto taking us into the Nordic landscapes of forests and winters and revealing to us the composer's preoccupation with nature. He described Sibelius conveying his experiences of synesthesia by conjuring pictures relating to "the serenity of water and woods, the awe of rocky heights, and the brooding mysticism these inspire."[52] The concerto, he wrote, offers images of "a swan moving on serene waters, a light-house with the reflection of its light on the water, of legendary giants throwing rocks and thunderbolts," and the violinist "paints the faces of nature" with the bow and lets the fingers "speak," to create the work's "kaleidoscopic moods and colors."[53]

Bronstein sustained the metaphor of the swan by directing violinists to play with a "tranquil bow" so as to not disturb the surface of a calm lake.[54] The metaphor of the swan was fortuitous. It was associated with the fifth symphony, and both the fifth and sixth symphonies were bound together with the idea of a second violin concerto in Sibelius's compositional imagination. It is also linked with nature-based cosmologies relating to the realms of death and the subconscious. Bronstein combined the swan metaphor with technical directions deriving from a theory of violin vocality. His advice regarding the ascending figuration in measures 21 to 23 in the second movement (see music example 4.1) is that violinists might "use a flautato stroke continuing the sense of flow in the whole arm, the separations almost unnoticeable. . . . On the notes leading into [measure] 23, hesitate slightly on

the last two notes, playing these with great melancholy
and depth, supporting the sound with a tightening of
the diaphragm."[55] He recommended that players pay
careful attention to bow distribution (what length of the
bow a player uses for each note) in the dance-like third
movement.[56]

Auer's teaching practice coincided with the emerging
political voices of women, and he accepted many women
violinists into his class in the St. Petersburg Conservatory,
who in turn went on to champion Sibelius's violin concerto internationally. Auer taught Cecilia Hansen, who
performed the concerto in Manchester with the Hallé
Orchestra in December 1935, and Maud Powell, who
played the American premiere. The Canadian violinist
Kathleen Parlow, who achieved recognition with her
London tours, was the first female violinist to enroll at the
St. Petersburg Conservatory. She described her lessons,
which were intensive and included individual and class
tuition. Auer's plan for daily practice (ideally no longer
than four hours of concentrated work) began with technical exercises (scales and studies) followed by the study
of compositions. Parlow noted that Auer helped his
students to develop technical skills and accurate intona-
tion by focusing on scales and by requiring them to practice slowly.[57]

The labor of twentieth-century women virtuosos raises issues around the gendered experiences of virtuosity. Sometimes, the judgments of their performances were based entirely on non-musical criteria. Flesch, for example, mentioned Sophia Jaffé, a Russian violinist who was his "one serious rival" during his studies, and he commented that he found her "outwardly unattractive," but "as a talent she was among the elite."[58] Flesch judged her to be "the greatest woman virtuoso of her time," though he tempered his judgment with the further comment that she was not "the most musical of violinists."[59] Her career on the concert stage was short. In another example of gendered judgment, Flesch wrote that he "would rather see than hear" Cecilia Hansen (⊙ see audio-visual example 4.9 on the website),[60] who was "one of the very few violinists whose posture and movements correspond to the laws of perfect physical harmony."[61] As recently as 1982, in a book about master violinists, Henry Roth devoted only one chapter to "women and the violin," after a series of chapters that each focused on a specific male player (Ysaÿe, Kubelik, Thibaud, etc.). His bias against women violinists is all too clear. Roth admitted that by the beginning of the twentieth century, it was "increasingly difficult, and often impossible, for even experienced professional competition judges to tell the difference between gifted male and female contestants," especially in blind auditions.[62] He insisted, however, that women did not reach the level of the greatest male violinists, expressing his belief that "the bone structure, plus the breadth, thickness and distribution of meat on the left hand finger-tip pads of *individual* men give them an

advantage in producing the ultimate resonance and rich-
ness . . . of tone."[63]

Despite such discriminatory attitudes, women violinists
managed to pursue successful solo and orchestral careers.
They changed ideas about musical ability based on gender
with their performances of works like Sibelius's violin
concerto. From the Finnish context, Anja Ignatius is still
recognized as one of the main early interpreters of this
concerto. In addition, less well-known violinists like Kerttu
Wanne pioneered women's professional musical paths.
Wanne was a successful principal player of the Turku City
Orchestra, appointed to this post in 1927, and became the
first Finnish female violinist to perform Sibelius's concerto
in that same year.[64] She began undertaking concert tours
as a soloist in Finland and internationally the following
year, including tours to Budapest in 1936 and four tours to
the United States, as well as a performance as soloist with
the Gothenburg Symphony Orchestra in 1942. She kept
notebooks with her program planning notes, indicating
that she continued to perform Sibelius's concerto, as well as
his other violin works, on her tours.[65] Wanne, like Ignatius,
Powell, and Parlow, was among those violinists whose
careers unfolded as women charted a place for themselves
on concert platforms and strove toward gender equality.
Their careers show that performing traditions are formed
by social considerations as well as by musical lineages (that
is, with whom a violinist studies), stylistic transmission,
and patterns of mobility. The advent of recording technology has provided a view of performing traditions and
violin virtuosity over the course of the twentieth century.

It coincided with greater acknowledgment of women virtuosos in the professional music marketplace, providing soundtracks to a democratic politics engaging with social equality, universal suffrage, and the gendered dimensions of labor.

CHAPTER 5

THE VIOLIN CONCERTO ON RECORD

J ASCHA HEIFETZ RECORDED SIBELIUS'S Violin
Concerto in D Minor (op. 47) in 1935 with the London
Philharmonic conducted by Sir Thomas Beecham at the
EMI Abbey Road Studio (⊙ see audio-visual example 5.1 on
the website).[1] This was a key moment in the history of this
work on record, establishing it as core repertory for virtuoso
violinists. Even the violinist Flesch, the harshest of critics
when it came to judging his peers, was moved by it. While
he considered Heifetz to be a violinist with "technical read-
iness," he criticized what he regarded as his tendency toward "unmotivated decrescendo in cantilena down-bows"
and "monotonous use of portamento"—an audible slide
from one note to another.[2] Yet he wrote that Heifetz's instrumental capacities were so great that he could play with

Jean Sibelius's Violin Concerto. Tina K. Ramnarine, Oxford University Press (2020). © Oxford University Press.
DOI: 10.1093/oso/9780190611538.001.0001

his mind at rest like "a Sleeping Beauty," and when "it was roused by the Prince of Inspiration, a work of art of the very first rank came into being, such as his interpretation of the Sibelius Concerto, to whose transcendental qualities the gramophone record bears witness."[3]

Heifetz makes expressive use of portamento in the 1935 recording, as did Tossy Spivakovsky in his later, and similarly acclaimed, 1959 version.[4] These examples are interesting given that recording technology affected playing styles, particularly with regard to choice of tempi and the decline of portamento as an expressive technical device.[5] Heifetz combined portamento with rhythmic precision, clear articulation in rapid figurations, and a Kajanus-like sense of forward momentum to generate a strong image of the work's structural proportions. He sustained his tempo choices toward the very final notes of each movement, thereby lending greater inevitability to their musical conclusions. His interpretation of the second movement is expansive but not too slow, and the third movement is one of the most exhilarating on record in terms of tempo, dramatic arch, and a playful character suggested by contrasting bowing techniques, and especially by the use of spiccato, an off-string articulation achieved by slightly bouncing the bow. Most striking is the interplay between the soloist and the orchestra, which is accentuated at moments that could have focused on the display of virtuosic capacity alone. For example, Heifetz lets the woodwind melodic lines take the foreground toward the end of the first movement by rendering the soloist's rapid string crossings as accompanying harmonic decoration (measures 441–58). In the second movement, the soloist retreats when the woodwind and the horns restate the opening melody, especially in accompanying (with rising broken octave patterns in the solo line) the melodic elaboration of a descending fourth in the clarinets, bassoons, and oboes (measures 49–52). Heifetz's interpretation emphasizes the co-sharing of the main melodic ideas in this movement, which is integral to Sibelius's re-conceptualization of the relationship between the soloist and orchestra.

Heifetz visited Sibelius at his home in Finland because, as one of his students, Ayke Agus reported, "He loved the Sibelius violin concerto and wanted to gather impressions for its authentic performance."[6] These impressions included the "austerity of the landscape," the forests, and the fog over the lakes, and Heifetz decided, "even before talking to Sibelius, that his interpretation of the violin concerto should somehow reflect this first impression"; but although Heifetz gave lengthy explanations about this concerto to his students later on, it was unclear how much these were based on Sibelius's advice.[7] He included this work as one of the possible audition pieces for players hoping to join his class at the University of Southern California, further indicating Heifetz's impact in shaping responses to Sibelius's concerto through his teaching practices as well as his recording.

Heifetz's 1935 recording is regarded by many violinists as setting the defining standard in the interpretation of Sibelius's concerto. (He made a second recording of the concerto, which was released in 1960, and a 1951 live recording with the New York Philharmonic has been restored and made available online; ⊙ see audio-visual example 5.2 on the website.)[8] In terms of performing traditions, it is located within the legacies of violin playing in imperial Russia's western borderlands (from which both Heifetz and Sibelius emerged), as well as within klezmer influences in both St. Petersburg and Auer's class at the conservatory. It shows none of the supposed deficiencies identified by Flesch, who wrote disparagingly (despite his own insistence on technical foundation as the ideal for musical interpretation) that Auer emphasized technique rather than musical considerations.[9] His description of a "typical" Auer pupil is a player who "values sensuous sonority and an attractive smoothness of tone much more highly than the difference between strong and weak beats and the shaping of musical ideas as such," and these were shortcomings that meant Auer failed to reach his potential as the greatest violin teacher of "all times."[10] Heifetz's recording testified to his abilities as a virtuoso and to his teacher's capacity to encourage his students to think individually about interpretation, style, and musical relevance. He was such a widely recognized violinist (see photograph 5.1) that he appeared in a 1939 film as himself (*They Shall Have Music*),[11] and a documentary was made about him in 2011, titled *God's Fiddler: Jascha Heifetz*.[12]

Sibelius's works were well received in America and Britain. The Finnish state, recognizing the potential of records to cement the international status of Finland's best-known musical figure, promoted public knowledge about Finnish cultural life by financially supporting the Columbia Gramophone Company recordings of Sibelius's first and second symphonies performed by the London Symphony Orchestra and conducted by Robert Kajanus in 1930. In 1932, the London Symphony Orchestra and the

PHOTOGRAPH 5.1   A photograph of the Russian American violinist Jascha
Heifetz (1901–87) in 1917. From the Bain News Service
photograph collection, held in the Library of Congress
Prints and Photographs Division, Washington, DC.

Royal Philharmonic Orchestra began a series of recordings
of Sibelius's symphonies conducted by Kajanus with the
London-based His Master's Voice. By 1936 all of Sibelius's
symphonies were available on records issued by RCA
Victor and Columbia Gramophone Company. Among
various performers were the Boston Symphony Orchestra
conducted by Sergei Koussevitzky. One of Sibelius's most
ardent promoters in America was the music critic Olin
Downes. He viewed the benefits of technological media
in terms of cultural access and "democratic right,"[13] and
he hoped that everyone would hear classical music, using

the radio as a medium to develop music appreciation. In commentaries for radio performances of Sibelius's works given by the Boston Symphony and the New York Philharmonic orchestras between 1930 and 1933, he described the composer as "the last of the heroes," whose works evoked in him a wish "to set out in oilskins, or something, for somewhere, to discover at least a desperate polar bear bent on conflict."[14] By contrast, the social philosopher and critic Theodor W. Adorno wrote dismissively about both Sibelius's popularity and the mass dissemination of cultural artifacts through audio technologies. Sibelius was a heroic figure for Downes but the abhorrent center of a personality cult for Adorno, who also saw the radio as a commodity marker that enabled recognition of tunes rather than real musical knowledge.[15]

Audio technologies provide greater cultural access, but they cannot capture the full musical experience of the live event. They provide a disembodied listening experience. Disembodiment intersects with nineteenth- and early twentieth-century violinists' pedagogic ideals about the singing qualities of the instrument as an embodiment of a performer's metaphysical essence or vitality.[16] It is a topic that absorbed violinists as they began to turn to the new recording technologies and to comment on the quality of the replication. Maud Powell, a violinist Sibelius admired, became the first instrumentalist to record for the Victor Talking Machine Company's celebrity series, the Red Seal label, in 1904, although there is no recording of her performance of Sibelius's violin concerto. Early recording technology, made on wax, only allowed the capture of a few minutes of a performance, but Powell welcomed it as a way of disseminating the violin repertoire. A musician had to stand as close as possible to the recording device. Powell said: "I am never as frightened as I am when I stand in front of that horn to play. There's a ghastly feeling that you're playing for all the world and an awful sense that what is done *is* done."[17] Flesch began recording on Edison machines in 1905, playing on the Stroh violin (a string instrument combined with an attached horn and mechanically amplified by a metal resonator). In view of its technological limitations, he believed that recordings would not be a long-lasting medium for musical transmission, since posterity would not be able to judge musicians' performances accurately. There is no recording of Flesch's interpretation of Sibelius's concerto. But he thought about this work when commenting on improvements in recording technology that captured the performance qualities of violinists like Heifetz more effectively. He still regarded records as having limited educational value:

> If I were to advise a pupil who is studying, say, the Sibelius Concerto, to listen to Heifetz's exemplary recording, he would, as we know from experience, try above all to imitate the virtuoso's manner, and thus be in danger of nipping in the bud the development of his own personality, even if he succeeded in occasionally assimilating devices of minor importance. . . . The great interpretation, born of individual feeling, must needs be immediate, spontaneous and unique.[18]

Since Sibelius's compositional career coincided with the development of recording technology, there is a rich legacy facilitating the comparison of different recorded interpretations of his concerto, during and after his lifetime.

By the 1970s, there were already around forty commercial examples, although many of the violinists involved in the early transmission of this work, for example, Flesch, Powell, and Vécsey, were not recorded playing it. A broad insight into their performing styles is possible from listening to the other works they recorded. Rather than surveying as many recordings as possible, this discussion focuses on some examples that connect with the themes of historical interest, biography, and the child prodigy.

The first Finnish violinist to record the work was Anja Ignatius (see photograph 5.2), a student of Flesch, who enjoyed an international concert career. She recorded it

PHOTOGRAPH 5.2   A photograph of the Finnish violinist Anja Ignatius (1911–95). Reproduced with permission from the Sibelius Museum / Stiftelsen för Åbo Akademi, Finland.

in 1943 in Berlin with Sibelius's brother-in-law, Armas Järnefelt, conducting the Städtisches Orchester Berlin (⏵ see audio-visual example 5.3 on the website).[19] Ignatius also performed the concerto with the Radio Symphony Orchestra for the final concert at the 1952 Olympic Games held in Helsinki (⏵ see audio-visual example 5.4 on the website).[20]

Another Finnish violinist, Heimo Haitto, recorded the concerto with Paavo Berglund conducting the Finnish Radio Symphony Orchestra in 1964, a recording that was re-released in 2013.[21] Ignatius's and Haitto's recordings offer an interpretative detail from the composer's perspective. Ignatius had already recorded the concerto when Sibelius asked her to avoid a ritenuto, a slight slowing down in the third movement just before the final section of intricate passagework (measure 209).[22] His comment is a rare interpretative insight showing that he envisioned a precise rhythmic execution for the concerto's ending. Haitto studied the concerto with Boris Sirpo, who had been in dialogue with Sibelius about how the work might be played, and one might speculate that his recording implicitly suggested some performing insights offered by the composer. Haitto maintained more rhythmic consistency in his interpretation of the third movement, in keeping with Sibelius's comment, as did Heifetz in his 1935 recording, although Sibelius selected Ignatius's tempo choice as the ideal one when he eventually added a metronome marking. In her violin teaching practice, Ignatius emphasized the rhythmic precision and consistency of Sibelius's violin concerto. The Finnish conductor Jukka-Pekka Saraste, who studied violin with Ignatius, noted that she was very strict about rhythm;

for example, she insisted that the second movement should be played with absolutely no rubato (variations in the tempo). It is not clear if this performance direction comes directly from Sibelius or whether it is Ignatius's mediation, but Saraste comments that as a conductor he is aware that the tempo in the slow movement should not change, and that there is even a steadiness in the instrumentation. As a conductor, he feels most comfortable working with a soloist who understands the concerto's uncompromising rhythmic precision. As a conductor, too, Saraste offers a further insight into interpretative issues. He noted that orchestras are sometimes wary of playing the ricochet bowing (the effect of dropping the bow at the tip onto the string) in the string accompaniment to the opening theme of the third movement. The wariness of players stems from viewing the movement as macabre in character, but the ricochet is, in fact, an essential color.[23] The re-released historical recordings of Haitto, Heifetz, and Ignatius have been uploaded to the internet. A modern aesthetics of precision means that contemporary recordings often demonstrate the kind of rhythmic vigor that Sibelius indicated as being part of his conceptualization. One of the most impressive in this respect is the Norwegian violinist Vilde Frang's 2010 debut recording. Although she hesitates slightly at the particular points where Sibelius imagined forward momentum, her technical ease and lightness of touch emphasize the dance-like character of this movement.[24]

Sibelius valued interpretations of his concerto by violinists from different schools. Ida Haendel (born in 1928 in Chelm, Poland) was a student of Flesch and Georges Enescu, the violinist and composer who spent some time studying in

Paris and also taught Yehudi Menuhin. She received a letter of thanks from the composer for her interpretation of the concerto, which she performed in Helsinki with the Radio Symphony Orchestra in 1949. Sibelius wrote: "Please accept my most cordial thanks for your excellent performance of my Violin Concerto. You played it masterfully in every respect. I congratulate you upon the great success. But above all I congratulate myself that my Concerto has found an interpreter of your rare standard."[25] The letter became one of Haendel's "most treasured possessions," as she wrote in her autobiography,[26] a sentiment she repeated over thirty years later in a 2004 documentary film, *I Am the Violin* (⊙ see audio-visual example 5.5 on the website).[27] Of several recordings she made of the concerto, her favorite was a live 1993 performance with Simon Rattle conducting the City of Birmingham Symphony Orchestra, which the BBC released in a 1996 album entitled *Testament*.[28]

What is the labor of virtuosity when we consider the child prodigy? Heifetz, Haendel, and Haitto all displayed an immediate empathy with the violin as child virtuosos. They all developed the discipline of practice. Haendel writes that music was "drilled" into her consciousness early during her elder sister's lessons. She explains her first performance, as a three-and-a-half-year-old child looking for something to do:

> I announce firmly . . . "I can play the song you are singing, Mama!" . . . I put the violin under my chin, but it was much too large for me. I found an alternative by placing my chin not on the chin rest but lower down. Without looking for the notes, I began to play the song as if I had played it a thousand times.[29]

In an international concert career, Haendel encountered such contemporary luminaries as Huberman, Flesch, Enescu, Heifetz, Menuhin, Josef Hassid, and Isaac Stern, among others. In her memoirs, she compared the insights she had gained from Flesch and Enescu. The former was born to be a teacher and ran his lessons in public with a "methodical, clinical, well-organised approach,"[30] and the latter made suggestions, never seeming to impose his own ideas. Indeed, Flesch wrote about a discipline of practice based on analyzing useful tasks, rather than on quantity of time spent in violin playing. He called this the "science of study," and he focused on building a player's dexterity through "applied technique" as a foundation for thinking about musical interpretation.[31] As Enescu's student, Haendel wrote, she rarely "had the chance to perform a work without interruptions and corrections at every bar and phrase," nor did Enescu often "illustrate his ideas on the violin—all was done verbally or on the piano."[32]

Her comments on the French violinist Ginette Neveu, one of her fellow students, dwelled on the limited opportunities for women concert violinists in the first half of the twentieth century. Despite Haendel's admiration for Neveu, she expressed some reservation when their concert tours in America coincided. As she wrote, "Two renowned violinists of the same sex bursting in on the New York musical scene practically simultaneously. We didn't consider that Ginette and I were rivals in the true sense—there was nearly a decade separating our ages, and our playing differed as day from night; but there was no getting away from the fact that we were both woman violinists."[33] Neveu helped to popularize Sibelius's violin concerto with her 1946 recording with the Philharmonia, conducted by Walter Susskind, which was made by EMI Records in London. The recording is still highly esteemed for its expressive intensity. According to Salmenhaara, however, Sibelius did not like Neveu's interpretation of the final movement because of the slow tempo.[34] Sibelius had written to his publisher, in 1941, that "the best virtuosi play ca. 108–116 to make *das virtuose* stand out."[35] Neveu was killed tragically in an airplane crash in 1949, a year after she toured Australia with Sibelius's concerto.

Gendered thinking was so deeply ingrained in Haendel's psyche that she conformed to prevalent ideas about the superior qualities of male virtuosity and the violin as a "masculine instrument," as she wrote, "requiring masculine treatment."[36] Her ideas about masculinity and violin playing as applied to interpreting Sibelius's violin concerto could only have been exacerbated by Downes's popular image of the composer as a virile, Viking-like figure.[37] Haendel represented herself as not feeling "graceful or feminine" when playing the violin, further adding that she herself disliked seeing women violinists (with the exception of Neveu), since most treated the violin "as a delicate toy, forgetting its great potential, or, aiming for masculinity, make it sound brutally harsh and percussive, more like chopping wood than music."[38] Crucially, sociopolitical circumstances prompted her wish to avoid giving an impression of femininity. Only when she was not playing did she want to be "as womanly as possible," and she struggled with the divide between public virtuoso and private life, admitting that "such a drastic transformation was, and is, difficult to achieve."[39] She wished to consult Neveu about the public and private divide, but she could not presume to do so, noting only, "We were in the same boat; both violinists of international repute, and both women. I so desperately wanted to have the best of both worlds and I wondered how Ginette felt about the problem."[40] Throughout her professional life, Haendel has been deeply aware of her limited opportunities as a woman violinist, which extended to differences in payment.[41] She commented in the 2004 documentary on concert invitations over the course of her career, during which time women violinists became increasingly successful in orchestras and competitions (⊙ see audio-visual example 5.5). Haendel, who began a performing career in the 1930s as a child prodigy, is being rediscovered by a new generation of violinists through her ongoing pedagogic work, as well as through virtual technologies and documentary photographs of her at the age of eighty-nine by Jelle Pieter de Boer (see photograph 5.3). Yet she now notes another hurdle in the predominant tendency to employ young musicians, showing that gender and age biases intersect in the concert hall. Issues about equality have not been resolved in the contemporary world of work—musical or otherwise.

Haendel reflected too on virtuosity as affective labor, noting interpretative advice offered by the conductor Sergiu Celibidache. He commented that "one should never run away with emotions. When you feel carried away, this is when you should keep yourself in check. . . . If you see a crescendo it doesn't mean that you have to make an accelerando." Haendel also understood the dictum of "not running away" as a technique "to stretch and expand beautiful themes."[42] It is a technique that can be applied to the very

PHOTOGRAPH 5.3   A photograph of the Polish-born violinist Ida Haendel by
the portrait and documentary photographer Jelle Pieter de
Boer. It is part of the series "Ida." The original is in color.
Reproduced with permission from Jelle Pieter de Boer.

opening of Sibelius's violin concerto. Both Haendel's and
Neveu's recordings of Sibelius's violin concerto illustrate
a sense of expansiveness in their treatment of the work's
lyrical themes. This sense of expansion characterized
Haendel's discourse on this concerto; she spoke about its
"philosophical contemplation," the time taken "to dream,"
and its sublime melodies that "soar into heaven."[43]

Sibelius also admired Heimo Haitto, who began his career as a child prodigy in Finland, and whose performances
were shaped by the diverse musical practices that traversed
the Finnish and Russian border. When he toured Canada
and the United States as a young violinist at the time of the
Finnish Winter War (1939–40), critics compared him to
Menuhin. He was born into a family of violinists; his father

was his first teacher, who guided him through scales, taught him to read notation, and instructed him to play Kreutzer's études, and his mother often played the mandolin for him. Haitto published an autobiography with recollections of asking his father to let him play the violin when he was two and a half years old. His father said, "If you manage to play on the different strings without touching the others at the same time with the bow, then you can begin to play."[44] Haitto described his excitement and also his surprise that it was more difficult than he had imagined to play on just one string. He began serious study at the age of five. When he turned nine, his parents asked a well-known Finnish violinist (not named in Haitto's autobiography) if he had the potential to become a student of Boris Sirpo in Vyborg (Viipuri in Finnish). An affirmative response led the family to travel from the west to the east of Finland, where Haitto auditioned successfully for a place to study at the Vyborg Conservatory. In his audition with Sirpo, Haitto was asked to play all the scales in three octaves before turning to his audition piece, Vittorio Monti's *Csárdás*. The audition was followed by a visit to Sirpo's home, and, after a discussion, Haitto's father told him that he would be staying there until the age of eighteen. It was undoubtedly a practical arrangement, as there would have been no possibility of commuting from Haitto's home town of Tornio in the northwest of Finland.

Sirpo instructed Haitto in the violin and became his foster father. Haitto also studied orchestral and operatic repertoire, conducting, and composing. He began a rigorous violin practice schedule of six hours a day. Days of rest were spent at Sirpo's country home, where Haitto played with Leo, Sirpo's son, who was two years older than him. Haitto gave an account of Vyborg as an important musical center, which many renowned performers visited from across Europe. One of these was the violinist Henry Temijanka, who performed Tchaikovsky's violin concerto with the Vyborg Orchestra. Temijanka stayed at Sirpo's home, and Haitto listened to him preparing, amazed that this violinist could focus on one bar of the work for half a day's practice. Later, both violinists met again in Hollywood and spent much time playing together in a string quartet.[45] By his twelfth year, Haitto was studying the virtuoso repertoire, reading a book about Paganini (who often appeared in his dreams thereafter) and studying one of his concertos. Haitto cherished this time in his life with its daily three-hour violin lessons followed by walks around Vyborg with Sirpo.

Playing Sirpo's Guarneri violin, Haitto made his debut as a soloist at age thirteen with the Helsinki Philharmonic Orchestra conducted by his teacher. He was then invited to appear as soloist with the Finnish Radio Symphony Orchestra, though he felt he had played wretchedly (*kurjasti*). As he was sobbing in his dressing room afterward, the telephone rang, and he heard somebody say, "I would like to speak to Heimo." The violinist heard himself responding between his sobs, "It's me"—upon which the voice continued: "It is Jean Sibelius speaking here. I wanted to thank you for your fine performance, which I have just heard on the radio." Haitto reported that his sorrow vanished at that moment, and that he felt privileged that "our great master" had taken the trouble to telephone him.[46] A few days later Haitto was invited to participate in a violin competition organized by the British

Council in London, although he was slightly younger than the minimum entry age of fourteen years. He had an opportunity to try out violins made by Stradivarius, Guarneri, and Guadagnini at the Hill and Son Company. He won the competition. The following day, Sirpo gave him new works to study, including the Sibelius violin concerto, although unfortunately Haitto did not provide any further details about his study of this work. By the age of sixteen, he was performing the concerto in the United States.

Following widespread critical acclaim, Haitto migrated to the United States in 1939 with Sirpo, escaping the Russian invasion of Finland. They traveled via Sweden and Norway, where Haitto gave concerts to raise funds for the Finnish Red Cross. Both continued to fundraise with concerts in the United States and Canada. Haitto performed concerts with Eugene Ormandy and the Philadelphia Orchestra, among others. He appeared in the 1941 film *There's Magic in Music* (⊙ see audio-visual example 5.6 on the website),[47] and he continued his violin studies with Louis Persinger and Ivan Galamian during his service in the US Navy.

Afterward, Haitto found employment in a studio orchestra, and then in the Los Angeles Philharmonic. He returned to Finland for a concert tour in 1948 and appeared in another film, *Pikku Pelimannista Viulun Kuninkaaksi* [The little fiddler becomes the king of the violin].[48] Haitto also worked as an orchestral violinist with several ensembles, including the Seattle Symphony Orchestra, the Bellas Artes Orchestra of Mexico City, the Metropolitan Opera Orchestra, the Honolulu Symphony, the Savonlinna Symphony, and the Joensuu Symphony, as well as spending some years roaming aimlessly, including on the beaches of California, before a teaching career at the Lahti Conservatory of Music (1963, where one of his students was the conductor Jukka-Pekka Saraste),[49] and writing his memoirs.[50]

Haitto's career has been assessed as having been partially wasted; there are few recorded examples of his playing even though he was considered to be a violinist at the level of Heifetz,[51] so his recording of Sibelius's violin concerto is all the more significant. He enjoyed playing the work most with Paavo Berglund, with whom he recorded it; they held a mutual regard for each other's musicianship. By studying with Sirpo he gained some insights into Sibelius's conception of the work, and he benefited from his teacher's transnational musical experiences. Sirpo was born in Vladikavkaz in Russia and studied violin and conducting at the conservatories in Moscow and in St. Petersburg. Following further study in Germany and Austria, he moved to Helsinki in 1912 to assume a position as violinist in the Helsinki Philharmonic. From 1918 to 1939, he was the director of the music school he established in Vyborg, and he conducted performances with the Vyborg Symphony Orchestra, rehearsing for one conducted by Sibelius in 1923.[52] Sibelius had a long connection with Vyborg, visiting his brother-in-law, the conductor Armas Järnefelt, there.[53] After Sirpo moved to the United States, he established the Portland Chamber Orchestra in 1947, which he directed until his death. He held teaching appointments, notably with Lewis and Clark College, and he developed a summer music festival. He continued to program Sibelius's works, thereby contributing to the composer's popularity in the United States.

Contextual information helps listeners compare different interpretations of the concerto. Listeners make personal aesthetic judgments without necessarily reaching agreement. "What is the best recording of Sibelius's concerto?" This question, posted on an online discussion group for violinists, generated many nominations over a period of five years while the thread was live.[54] Heifetz, Haendel, Kavakos, Neveu, Oistrakh, Chang, Spivakovsky, and Vengerov were among those nominated. In comparing recordings such as these, listeners can also gain knowledge of the performing traditions transmitted through them. In contrast to this kind of performance knowledge, philosophical discussion has been more interested in the status of the record as an industrial artifact in mass production and popular culture.

Records occupy the theoretical imagination precisely because they reveal musical and social processes. In the twenty-first century, virtuosity is seen as being embedded in cultural industries as a form of self-presentation, and virtuosity risks being confined to celebrity culture in the domains of industrial production and technologies of mass reproduction. From the perspective of musical transmission, however, records are instrumental in analyzing the history of performing traditions from the twentieth century onward. They show how female virtuosos carved out a new vista of gender equality through sonic artifacts, including the recordings of Sibelius's violin concerto. The recording, juxtaposed with film (documentary and fictional) and autobiographical writing (including the examples by Auer, Flesch, Haendel, and Haitto), provides an archive of virtuosity as a practice and a sociopolitical phenomenon.

CHAPTER 6

LEGACIES

WHEN SIBELIUS WAS CELEBRATING his ninetieth birthday, he invited the violinist Yehudi Menuhin to play his concerto, the work that so intimately captured Sibelius's own earliest musical aspirations, in Helsinki. Almost a decade later, in July 1964, Menuhin wrote about his memories of the composer "looking like one of the oldest trees" among the forests surrounding Ainola.[1] Menuhin's description is apt because it evokes the broad context of the forest cultures within which Sibelius's compositions are situated, and it assumes a new significance in our era of concern about the environment. Menuhin's description fits within an ecological reading of the Sibelius violin concerto, musical tradition, and virtuosity.

Jean Sibelius's Violin Concerto. Tina K. Ramnarine, Oxford University Press (2020). © Oxford University Press.
DOI: 10.1093/oso/9780190611538.001.0001

Sibelius's violin concerto offers a lesson on the labor of virtuosity, the formation of performing traditions over time, and musical imagination. The lesson begins with a presentation of skill (on the musical page, onstage, and on record) and concludes with a broad view of musical communication. The image of the nineteenth-century virtuoso as sorcerer reappears on the twenty-first-century stage as a bearer of tradition, whose performances are magically multiplied in the virtual arena. Virtuosity remains a distant horizon without effort, without labor. In Marx's terms, this labor is characterized by the value attached to it through the exchange of capital. This is virtuosity as the branding and selling of celebrity. In pedagogical terms, regarding the violin, this labor is a highly disciplined, embodied practice that seeks its raison d'être in the multiplicity of interpretative possibilities. This is virtuosity as an exploration of the musical imagination. In terms of the child prodigy, labor is play.

For Sibelius, the labor of virtuosity was a struggle and a divine inspiration; recall the image of the performer-composer overflowing with ideas, unable to tear himself away from the marvelous music he played. Sibelius's labor, especially in relation to the virtuoso's role, is revealed by comparing both versions of his concerto. The soloist in the first version has more to play. In revising the concerto, Sibelius went beyond editorial corrections to reach a "new conception of the work," in which he reconsidered the virtuoso's role and sought a greater integration of the cadenzas within the overall structure.[2] Sibelius's friend Carpelan offered advice on this matter in December 1903. He asked if the technical challenges of the concluding cadenza of the second movement were necessary, and he noted that its rapid figuration looked "too virtuoso after the heavenly thoughts of the movement."[3] Following his initial defense of the cadenza, Sibelius deleted it before the premiere, and it was never heard as part of the work. Such care is taken over the cadenza because it is crucial to conveying the virtuoso's authority and expertise. The cadenza emphasizes virtuosity by drawing on the Italian meanings of *virtù*: bravura, mimesis, and spontaneity. While bravura is "playing at the very edge of technique," mimesis astounds an audience by imitation (of nature sounds, other musical instruments, and the human voice), and spontaneity is related to improvisatory passages.[4] This way of looking at virtuosity brings a central problem in concerto writing into focus, which is the relationship between soloist and orchestra. Kalevi Aho writes about this problem with reference to his own violin concerto, commissioned and premiered by the Finnish Radio Symphony Orchestra in 1982: "How to give the soloist sufficient significant and virtuosic material without reducing the role of the orchestra to mere accompaniment. . . . The soloist and orchestra strive to be equal, complementary and mutually supporting elements."[5] Saraste spoke about the struggle between the soloist and the orchestra in the Sibelius violin concerto as part of its drama, observing that in the third movement, for example, the conductor has "to balance the struggle so that the orchestra is not only accompanying but also giving an element of contrast or confrontation to the soloist all the time."[6]

The relational aspects of a concerto bring *virtù*—as bravura, mimesis, and spontaneity—into play with moral and philosophical reflections on virtuosity construed as virtue, which is an idea founded on Enlightenment notions of will and intellect. Virtuosity as an expression of the will is the internal struggle between two tendencies in human nature, toward either good action or its opposite. It conveys a sense of mastering oneself in the unfolding of an internal moral struggle, one that is made public in the performance of *virtù*. A politics of possibility emerges because the element of risk within virtuosity is haunted by a moral drama played out on public stages with uncertain outcomes. Since this drama is configured as the display of disciplined and embodied human skill, it illustrates that the body becomes the site of political action, though it is also related to the display of skill within realms of sorcery that bring into visibility what would otherwise remain invisible. Contributing one act to this moral drama is a reading of Sibelius as a political figure in Finnish nationalism.[7] Such a reading has been one of the legacies of a scholarship in which Sibelius achieved the status of a Hegelian "great man," a profoundly important canonization that has shaped Finnish musicological discourse.[8] He was heralded as a modern-day Väinämöinen, a representation of the composer that summoned the greatest sorcerer in Finnish epic tradition, who had sung the ecological topography of the national landscape into existence.

The political context of Sibelius and his violin concerto brings the revolutionary potential of virtuosity to the fore, which lies in rethinking musical, human, and ecological relations. Virtuosity as a trope in relational thought is an aspiration for the most complementary expression of human exchanges, for an understanding of human moral differences that leads to Hegel's spiritual reconciliations.[9]

Aho's concept of mutual support provides a safe space for moral subjects (soloist and orchestra) aspiring to self-mastery in the presence of an audience. Indeed, audiences are active participants in the performance of this kind of aspiration. The concerto and the performance event are tools for reflecting on the imaginative, communicative, and political capacities we share with others.

Safe spaces are needed, since the failure of virtuosity onstage, however temporary, is unsettling, albeit sometimes inevitable. Viktoria Mullova, the winner of the 1980 Sibelius Violin Competition, who left the Soviet Union dramatically in the aftermath of that success to seek political asylum in the United States, spoke about preventing stage fright, and she advocated preparation in an online violin masterclass.[10] In a homemade video for the Philharmonia Orchestra, Pekka Kuusisto (see photograph 6.1), winner of the 1995 Sibelius Violin Competition, highlighted participatory performance. He invited audiences to participate in a communal experience of singing, playing, and dancing to traditional Nordic tunes.[11] This was based on the successful encore performance he gave at a BBC Proms concert in August 2016, in which everyone sang the chorus of a folk song in Finnish. The performance was posted on YouTube and was an immediate internet success (see the accompanying website for further discussion on violin pedagogy and well-being).[12] This sense of participation also stems from his artistic involvement with Our Festival, organized by Järvenpää's Sibelius Society, held in locations around Lake Tuusula, which seeks "new perspectives on musical encounters and concert practices."[13] At a BBC Proms concert in August 2019, Kuusisto extended audience

understandings of cross-genre connections in a performance of Sibelius's violin concerto with the BBC Scottish Symphony Orchestra, conducted by Thomas Dausgaard. For this performance, he invited the Finnish musicians Timo Alakotila, Taito Hoffrén, Ilona Korhonen, Minna-Liisa Tammela, and Vilma Timonen to collaborate in the performance of a prelude (composed and arranged by Alakotila and Dausgaard) to convey possible thematic connections between Finnish folk traditions and the concerto (see the accompanying website for further discussion on this performance). Both Mullova and Kuusisto have found safe performance spaces in the exploration of diverse musical traditions and playing styles. They follow the legacy of Sibelius's comparative and cross-genre interests, embracing the virtuoso concerto alongside the experimental ensemble work or the folk song. The revolutionary potential of virtuosity in this case is musical as well as political. It concerns embracing a wide range of musical genres to forge new understandings of the different ways in which musicians demonstrate mastery. In the twenty-first century, it is time to begin asking questions about how discourses on virtuosity operate to include or exclude, to make or unmake the virtuoso.

What are the compositional legacies of Sibelius's violin concerto in the Finnish context? Finnish composers have spoken about being in the shadow of Sibelius, although this has not deterred them from composing virtuoso violin concertos. Erkki Melartin's Violin Concerto in D Minor (op. 60) was composed in 1913. As with Sibelius's concerto, the violin solo enters in the first few bars with a lyrical melody, and its virtuosic writing includes double stops, rapid shifts of register, and a re-conceptualization of the cadenza. It is not widely performed, but it merits more attention, and now that it is available on YouTube, it attracts positive commentary.[14] Several other examples of the violin concerto were commissioned and premiered by the Finnish Broadcasting Company's Finnish Radio Symphony Orchestra, including those by Eero Hämeenniemi (1991), Pehr Henrik Nordgren (1977), Paavo Heininen (1999), Jyrki Linjama (2001), and Jouni Kaipainen (2006). The Finnish Radio Symphony also premiered Einojuhani Rautavaara's violin concerto (1977).[15] In the note for the score of her violin concerto *Graal Théâtre* (premiered in 1995), Kaija Saariaho writes about the tension she feels between her efforts as a composer and performance as theatre, especially when a soloist plays a major physical and musical role. Esa-Pekka Salonen's violin concerto (2008) is included as one of the music examples on a mobile app called the Orchestra (2012), allowing users to hear musicians' commentaries, listen to the work, and follow its score. Salonen emphasized the collaborative nature of concerto composition and performance, explaining his work with the soloist, Leila Josefowicz, via virtual technologies such as skype and email.

Digital environments enable violinists and the broader public to listen to many interpretations of Sibelius's violin concerto, and to the technical and musical suggestions of different players. The Sibelius Violin Competition, which was established in 1965 and became an important musical institution in the transmission of this work, has moved toward digital dissemination. The 2015 violin competition was the eleventh since its inception, and its winner, Christel Lee from the United States, was the soloist with the Finnish Radio Symphony Orchestra in a concert marking the 150th anniversary of Sibelius's birth. The anniversary year saw a record number of competition applicants: 234.[16]

Competitors in 2015, as well as other tourists, visited Ainola during the anniversary celebration. Perhaps they went in hope of communing with Sibelius's musical spirit, to sense the musical echoes still reverberating in his home. They also went to pay their respects. The Finnish state had granted special permission for Sibelius and Aino to be buried there, and Sibelius's funeral in 1957 revealed the extent to which the composer had become a national and international icon, with the attendance of heads of state from many countries, and crowds of people lining the streets. Today, Sibelius's home is a pilgrimage site, a heritage building that is an architectural embodiment of cultural memory. Santeri Levas, who was the personal secretary to the composer between 1938 and 1957, offered a memory of Sibelius's work space. He described the light, sunshine, and sense of spaciousness on the ground floor of Ainola. The drawing room served as the composer's work room; the "Third Symphony, the tone poems *Pohjola's Daughter* and *Night-ride and Sunrise*, the string quartet *Voces intimae*, the incidental music for August Strindberg's *Swanwhite*, and a considerable number of smaller works were written, and the Violin Concerto revised, here."[17]

Sibelius's home is now a heritage site. His violin concerto is also a work of cultural heritage although it is circulated widely, including through technological media that invite increasingly plural responses to the work of art. Musical transmission in a digital era decentralizes Hegel's idea of a universal truth and leaves the question of art's purpose open to new answers. The earliest recorded violinists expressed fears about the loss of live performance experiences and the death of original interpretations with the technological circulations of musical works. Now it is possible to see music transmission technologies as offering new kinds of participatory experiences that enrich the individual's sense of tradition, heritage, and the past. After all, histories of performing traditions inform performances in digital spaces. The media researcher Chris Salter notes that technology, art, and everyday life pose questions around aesthetic practices dealing with "real-life problems," and artists might "develop total and organic environments where the separation and dualities between vision and reality, image and environment could be dissolved."[18]

For the philosopher Immanuel Kant, these dualities can be dissolved by the power of the imagination. In *Anthropology from a Pragmatic Point of View*, a collection of lectures based on some of the earliest university teaching within the discipline of anthropology (notably replete with opinions and biases from a contemporary reading), Kant wrote that even a great artist or sorceress must get material from the senses. Thus, sensory perception seems to "provide a reality to its (invented) intuitions because of the analogy between them and real perceptions."[19] This is virtù as mimesis rather than a moral or philosophical discourse on virtue. It is the violin strings vibrating "beneath the stroke of the bow, in accordance with the same principles which cause the strings of an Aeolian harp to stir in the breath of the wind," as Auer wrote.[20]

Kant's anthropology of sensory perception and the creative imagination is relevant in an age of environmental crisis, including in terms of thinking about ecological music histories. Several biographers have commented on the natural environment in Sibelius's musical imagination. Levas reported specifically on birds and bird songs: "The flight of the migrant birds each spring and autumn was an important event for [Sibelius]. Everybody in Järvenpää knew that, and whenever swans or cranes came into sight he was immediately told—often by telephone. In earlier times he had taken long walks to see his favourite swans."[21] Levas reported that Sibelius could tell which starlings had listened to factory sirens, and that he heard the influence of the tones of Brazilian parrots in the music of Villa-Lobos.[22] In this respect, Sibelius demonstrated a keen sense of human hearing as dependent on sensory perception of the environment. Sound changes before we sense it, and the brain processes the vibrations entering the ears with an alertness to the continuously changing sounds of the natural world. Auer integrated his understanding of this biological phenomenon into his teaching by encouraging his students to develop their musical interpretations by listening creatively to nature.

Sibelius's violin concerto gives us insights into how performing traditions are formed through the practices of composers, performers, and institutions; through musicians' mobility and technological circulations; and through political processes and events. In portraying the time, locale, and cultural contexts of Sibelius's violin concerto, as well as performers' engagements with the work to the present day, this book has examined performing traditions within a wide range of practices that go beyond violin playing into different artistic and intellectual fields. It ends with the legacy of Sibelius's nature-based musical imagination, to which today's listeners are becoming increasingly sensitive, perhaps because we face the bleak realities of global environmental challenges. (Also see the accompanying website for further discussion on Sibelius's nature-based musical aesthetics.)

The violin itself speaks to these environmental challenges. Spruce forestry in Italy's Val di Fiemme is connected with sustainable resource management and also with Cremona's luthiers. These forests were managed carefully amid the demand for instruments and wood in the building of neighboring Venice's navy. *Lutherie* originally referred to the manufacturing of lutes. Craftsmen applied lute-making skills to bowed instruments of the violin family.[23] Violins made by Stradivarius were highly regarded in the eighteenth century and were mythologized as having unique properties in the nineteenth. Part of their value lies in violinists being able to trace the lineages of their instruments. Kreutzer's Stradivarius of 1727, for example, is played by Maxim Vengerov today. For the premiere of the revised version of Sibelius's violin concerto in Berlin, the Czech violinist Karel Halíř played Robert von Mendelssohn's Stradivarius of 1694–95, an instrument that is now called the Halir, and Vécsey had only just acquired his 1716 Maréchal Berthier Stradivarius when he gave his own first performance of Sibelius's work.[24] The value of a Stradivarius lies in its life history, beginning with its forest material and proceeding through a tradition of performance.[25] Indeed, this is the value of all violins, including Sibelius's Stainer and the homemade instruments fashioned out of local materials by players in Finland's interior forests.

Sibelius's ecologically oriented musical sensibility was foundational to his contemplation of violin virtuosity in the forest environment to which he moved when finalizing the concerto. It located him within Finno-Ugric forest cultures, and within the longer sonic histories of the boreal forests that emerged at the end of the Ice Age. In Ainola, Sibelius found that even "the silence speaks."[26] This, too, is beauty. This, too, is virtuosity. His musical imagination rests on the premise that humans are part of the polyvocality of nature. This is why he was so attentive to bird songs and forest sounds. Sibelius's violin concerto can be heard as part of a forest "jam-packed with non-human life, whose individual voices coalesce into an intense and collective symphony."[27] The *longue durée* of our sonic planet also belongs to an enquiry on the formation of performing traditions.

ADDITIONAL SOURCES
FOR READING AND
LISTENING

The original and revised versions of Sibelius's Violin Concerto in D Minor have been edited by the musicologist Timo Virtanen: *Jean Sibelius Works: Concerto for Violin and Orchestra Op. 47* (Wiesbaden: Breitkopf & Härtel, 2014). Facsimile reproductions of some of the sketches are included together with an illuminating essay about the composition of the concerto, the performances of the 1904 and 1905 versions, and the reception to them. He also writes about the Schnirlin edition of the solo violin part, which was published in 1929. This features fingerings, bowings, and metronome indications added by the violinist Ossip Schnirlin, although Sibelius's reactions to it are unknown. Virtanen gives an online lecture about this concerto, which is available on YouTube, https://www.youtube.com/watch?v=2FDZNolVcBg, accessed February 4, 2018, or ⊙ see audio-visual example 7 on the website.

Erkki Salmenhaara wrote about the violin concerto in a series on masterpieces of Nordic music: *Jean Sibelius Violin Concerto* (Wilhelmshaven, Germany: Florian Noetzel Verlag, 1996). Several biographies provide details on the cultural, social, and political contexts in which Sibelius worked. One of the best and most extensive is Erik Tawaststjerna's biography, edited and translated into English by Robert Layton. In its English-language version, it has been published in a set of three volumes: *Sibelius Volume I: 1865–1905* (London: Faber & Faber, 1976 [1965]); *Sibelius Volume II: 1904–1914* (London: Faber & Faber, 1986 [1972]); and *Sibelius Volume III: 1914–1957* (London: Faber & Faber, 2008 [1978]). Tomi Mäkelä's biography, *Jean Sibelius* (Woodbridge, UK: Boydell, 2011), includes details on Sibelius's violin concerto. Glenda Dawn Goss provides excellent details on the early stages of Sibelius's musical training in the biography *Sibelius: A Composer's Life and the Awakening of Finland* (Chicago: University of Chicago Press, 2009). A recent collection of essays on Sibelius's music more generally has been edited by Daniel M. Grimley, *Jean Sibelius and His World* (Princeton, NJ: Princeton University Press, 2011). For those interested in reading about the violin, one useful collection is *The Cambridge Companion to the Violin,* edited by Robin Stowell (Cambridge: Cambridge University Press, 1992), which includes the editor's own chapter on the nineteenth-century bravura tradition. Recordings of Sibelius's violin concerto are numerous, and the soloists of particular interest in relation to the discussion in this book include Sarah Chang, Vilde Frang, Ida Haendel, Heimo Haitto, Jascha Heifetz, Anja Ignatius, Leonidas Kavakos, Pekka Kuusisto, Yehudi Menuhin, Viktoria Mullova, Ginette Neveu, David Oistrakh, Tossy Spivakovsky, and Maxim Vengerov.

NOTES

CHAPTER 1

1 Ilmari Krohn, *Der Stimmungsgehalt der Symphonien von Jean Sibelius* (Helsinki: Der Finnischen Literaturgesellschaft, 1945), 229.
2 Cited in Karen A. Shaffer and Neva Garner Greenwood, *Maud Powell: Pioneer American Violinist* (Ames: Iowa State University Press, 1988), 237. The American premiere was performed with the New York Philharmonic and the Russian conductor Vasily Ilyich Safonov.
3 See "Vengerov: Sibelius (Violin Concerto)—'This Is Beauty,'" YouTube, https://www.youtube.com/watch?v=dk6tqaPLp5M, accessed June 5, 2017; or see audio visual example 1.1 on the website: Maxim Vengerov proclaims, "This is beauty."
4 Georg Wilhelm Friedrich Hegel, *Aesthetics: Lectures on Fine Art*, trans. T. M. Knox (Oxford: Clarendon, 1975 [1835]), 90.
5 Hegel 1975, 56–59.
6 Hegel 1975, 27.
7 Leo Tolstoy, *What Is Art?*, trans. Aylmer Maude (Kindle Edition, 2013 [1898]), 51.
8 Mai Kawabata, *Paganini: The "Demonic" Virtuoso* (Woodbridge, UK: Boydell, 2013).
9 Leopold Auer, *Violin Playing as I Teach It* (New York: Dover, 1980 [1921]), 70.
10 Bo Carpelan, *Axel*, trans. David McDuff (London: Paladin, 1991), 39.
11 See "Intervyu s Viktoriei Mullovoi // Interview with Viktoria Mullova (with subs)," YouTube, https://www.youtube.com/watch?v=o7iRwTMsnMs, accessed August 20, 2017; audio-visual example 1.2 on the website: Viktoria Mullova speaks about violin playing. Her reference to using gut strings for the Sibelius violin concerto is at 3:44.

12 Erik Tawaststjerna, *Sibelius Volume I: 1865–1905*, ed. and trans. Robert Layton (London: Faber & Faber, 1976 [1965]), 274.

13 See "Jean Sibelius as a Violinist," Jean Sibelius website, http://www.sibelius.fi/english/erikoisaiheet/ihmisena/ihm_02.htm, accessed August 20, 2017.

14 Santeri Levas, *Sibelius—A Personal Portrait* (London: J. M. Dent and Sons, 1972), 46.

15 Cited in Erik Tawaststjerna, *Sibelius Volume III: 1914–1957*, ed. and trans. Robert Layton (London: Faber & Faber, 2008), 18.

16 Hegel 1975, 29.

17 Anna-Maria von Bonsdorff, "Correspondences—Jean Sibelius in a Forest of Image and Myth," in *Sibelius and the World of Art*, ed. Hanna-Leena Paloposki (Helsinki: Ateneum Art Gallery, 2014), 95.

18 Jukka Tiilikainen, "The Genesis of the Violin Concerto," in *The Cambridge Companion to Sibelius*, ed. Daniel M. Grimley (Cambridge: Cambridge University Press, 2004), 73.

19 Levas 1972, 37.

20 Cited in Glenda Dawn Goss, *Sibelius: A Composer's Life and the Awakening of Finland* (Chicago: University of Chicago Press, 2009), 63.

21 Bengt de Törne, *Sibelius: A Close-Up* (London: Faber & Faber, 1937), 94.

22 Levas 1972, 49.

23 Auer 1980, 67.

24 Raphael Bronstein, *The Science of Violin Playing* (Brattleboro, VT: Echo Point Books and Media, 2016 [1977]), 119.

25 Cited in Tiilikainen 2004, 66.

26 Cited in Tawaststjerna 1976, 276.

27 Cited in Timo Virtanen, ed., *Jean Sibelius Works: Concerto for Violin and Orchestra Op. 47* (Wiesbaden, Germany: Breitkopf & Härtel, 2014), x.

28 Virtanen 2014, x.

29 Virtanen 2014, x.

30 Leonidas Kavakos, *Sibelius Violin Concerto op. 47*, original and final versions, Lahti Symphony Orchestra conducted by Osmo Vänskä, BIS, CD-500 (1991).

31 For example, see Hegel 1975, 74.

32 Jean Sibelius, "Joitakin Näkökohtia kansanmusiikista ja sen vaikutuksesta säveltaiteeseen," reproduced in *Musiikki* 2 (1980) [originally published 1896]: 86–105.

33 Goss 2009, 43.

34 George Nathaniel Curzon, *Russia in Central Asia in 1889 and the Anglo-Russian Question* (London: Longmans, Green, 1889).

35 Philip Longworth, *Russia's Empires: Their Rise and Fall from Prehistory to Putin* (London: John Murray, 2005), 216–22.

36 Juhani Aho, *Rautatie* [The railway] (Porvoo, Finland: Werner Söderström Osakeyhtiön Laakapaino, 1973 [1884]), 23, my translation.

37 J. R. Plunkett, "Some Famous Violinists," *Musical Opinion and Music Trade Review* 9 (100) (1886): 176.

38 Betty Weingartner, "August Wilhelmj," *Music and Letters* 32 (1) (1951): 101.

39 See "Jean Sibelius as a Violinist," Jean Sibelius website, http://www.sibelius.fi/english/erikoisaiheet/ihmisena/ihm_02.htm, accessed August 20, 2017.

40 Cited in Glenda Dawn Goss, *Jean Sibelius, The Hämeenlinna Letters: Scenes from a Musical Life, 1874–1895* (Esbo, Finland: Schildts Förlags, 1997), 47.

41 Satu Jalas, Lilli Paasikivi, and Folke Gräsbeck, *Ainola: Music by Jean Sibelius Performed on His Own Instruments*, Ainola Foundation, CD, Ainola-01 (2014).

42 Cited in Galina Kopytova, *Jascha Heifetz: Early Years in Russia* (Bloomington: Indiana University Press, 2014), 19.

43 Goss 1997, 78.

44 Goss 1997, 80.

45 Goss 1997, 81.

46 Goss 1997, 86.

47 Csillag, born in 1852 in Bakony-Telek, Hungary, became a member of the Court opera orchestra in Vienna. He later held orchestral positions as leader at Baden-Baden, Düsseldorf, Hamburg, and Rotterdam before teaching in Helsinki. See Carl Schroeder, *Handbook of Violin Playing*, trans. J. Matthews (London: Augener, 1920), p. 88.

48 Goss 1997, 89.

49 Goss 1997, 103.

50 Goss 1997, 84.

51 Letter to Pehr, June 7, 1888, cited in Goss 1997, 96.

52 Letter to Pehr, October 24, 1888, cited in Goss 1997, 99–100.

53 Letter to Pehr, February, 1888, cited in Goss 1997, 91.

54 Letter to Pehr, March 20, 1889, cited in Goss 1997, 104.

55 Goss 1997, 105.

56 Cited in Tawaststjerna 1976, 52.

57 Cited in Tawaststjerna 1976, 53.

58 Cited in Tawaststjerna 2008, 328.

59 Tawaststjerna 1976, 53.

60 Philip R. Bullock, "Sibelius and the Russian Traditions," in *Jean Sibelius and His World*, ed. Daniel M. Grimley (Princeton, NJ: Princeton University Press, 2011), 49.

61 Georg Wilhelm Friedrich Hegel, *Phenomenology of Spirit*, trans. A. V. Miller (Oxford: Oxford University Press, 1977 [1807]), 121.

62 Jacques Rancière, "Problems and Transformations in Critical Art," in *Participation: Documents of Contemporary Art*, ed. Claire Bishop (London: Whitechapel Gallery, 2006 [2004]), 83–93.

63 Timo Huusko, "Finlandia—from National Tableau to Triumphal Anthem," in *Sibelius and the World of Art*, ed. Hanna-Leena Paloposki (Helsinki: Ateneum Art Gallery, 2014), 255.

64 Eero Tarasti, "Jean Sibelius as an Icon of the Finns and Others: An Essay in Post-Colonial Analysis," in *Snow, Forest, Silence: The Finnish Tradition of Semiotics*, ed. Eero Tarasti (Bloomington: Indiana University Press, 1999), 221–46.

65 Stuart Hall, "For Allon White: Metaphors of Transformation," in *Stuart Hall: Critical Dialogues in Cultural Studies*, ed. David Morley and Kuan-Hsing Chen (London: Routledge, 1996), 288.

66 Maiko Kawabata, "Virtuoso Codes of Violin Performance: Power, Military Heroism, and Gender (1789–1830)," *19th-Century Music* 28 (2) (2004): 91.

67 Gabriel Banat, *The Chevalier de Saint-Georges: Virtuoso of the Sword and the Bow* (New York: Pendragon, 2006).

68 Kawabata 2004, 92.

69 Karl Marx, *Capital: Critique of Political Economy*, ed. Friedrich Engels, trans. Samuel Moore and Edward Aveling (Chicago: Aristeus, 2012 [1867]).

70 Karl Marx, *Theories of Surplus Value*, trans. G. A. Bonner and Emile Burns (London: Lawrence & Wishart, 1951), 27.

71 Marx 1951, 195.

72 Friedrich Nietzsche, *The Birth of Tragedy, and Other Writings*, ed. Raymond Geuss and Ronald Speirs, trans. Ronald Speirs (Cambridge: Cambridge University Press, 2007 [1871]), 40.

73 Paolo Virno, *A Grammar of the Multitude: For an Analysis of Contemporary Forms of Life*, trans. Isabella Bertoletti, James Cascaito, and Andrea Casson (South Pasadena, CA: Semiotext(e), 2004), 53.

74 Cited in Tawaststjerna 1976, 279.

CHAPTER 2

1 Cited in Hildi Hawkins and Soila Lehtonen, eds., *Helsinki: A Literary Companion* (Helsinki: Finnish Literature Society, 2000), 23.

2 Leonard C. Lundin, "Part Five: Finland," in *Russification in the Baltic Provinces and Finland, 1855–1914*, ed. Edward C. Thaden (Princeton, NJ: Princeton University Press, 1981), 365.

3 Hannu Salmi, *Wagner and Wagnerism in Nineteenth-Century Sweden, Finland, and the Baltic Provinces* (Rochester, NY: University of Rochester Press, 2005).

4 Antti Pajamo, "Well-Orchestrated Helsinki," *Finnish Music Quarterly* 1995 (1): 18.

5 Vesa Sirén, *Suomalaiset Kapellimestarit: Sibeliuksesta, Saloseen, Kajanuksesta Franckiin* (Helsinki: Otava, 2010), 28.

6 Eero Tarasti, "Finland among the Paradigms of National Anthems," in *Snow, Forest, Silence: The Finnish Tradition of Semiotics*, ed. Eero Tarasti (Bloomington: Indiana University Press, 1999), 110.

7 Sirén 2010, 28.

8 David Schoenbaum, *The Violin: A Social history of the World's Most Versatile Instrument* (New York and London: W. W. Norton, 2013), 295–307.

9 Salmi 2005, 212–14.

10 Vesa Kurkela, "Seriously Popular: Deconstructing Popular Orchestral Repertoire in Late Nineteenth-Century Finland," in *Critical Music Historiography: Probing Canons, Ideologies and Institutions*, ed. Vesa Kurkela and Markus Mantere (Farnham, UK: Ashgate, 2015), 135.

11 Kurkela 2015, 125.

12 Cited in Sirén 2010, 30.

13 In Helsinki's multilingual environment, both Finnish and Swedish were promoted by supporters known, respectively, as the Fennomans and the Svecomans.

14 Bullock 2011, 21–24.

15 Matti Huttunen, "The National Composer and the Idea of Finnishness: Sibelius and the Formation of Musical Style," in *The Cambridge Companion to Sibelius*, ed. Daniel M. Grimley (Cambridge: Cambridge University Press, 2004), 10.

16 Sirén 2010, 30–38.

17 Matti Vainio, *"Nouskaa Aatteet!" Robert Kajanus: Elämä ja Taide* (Helsinki: Werner Söderström Osakeyhtiö, 2002), 222–35.

18 Lauri Väkevä, "Music For All: Justifying the Two-Track Ideology of Finnish Music Education," in *Critical Music Historiography: Probing Canons, Ideologies and Institutions*, ed. Vesa Kurkela and Markus Mantere (Farnham: Ashgate, 2015), 46.

19 Cited in Väkevä 2015, 49.

20 Sirén 2010, 49–55.

21 Political and ecological interpretations of Sibelius's works were common in early Finnish musicology, which was intellectually situated within a broader field of scholarship focusing on the cultural and linguistic relations between Finns and other Finno-Ugric peoples. This scholarship provides an intellectual heritage that merits renewed scrutiny as political and ecological readings become prominent in music research once again.

22 Tomi Mäkelä, "Sibelius and Germany: *Wahrhaftigkeit* beyond *Allnatur*," in *The Cambridge Companion to Sibelius*, ed. Daniel M. Grimley (Cambridge: Cambridge University Press, 2004), 170.

23 Cited in Veijo Murtomäki, "Russian Influences on Sibelius," in *Proceedings from the Second International Conference on Sibelius, 1995*, ed. Veijo Murtomäki, Kari Kilpeläinen, and Risto Väisänen (Helsinki: Sibelius Academy, 1998), 155.

24 Maria Roditeleva, "Jean Sibelius—Seen by Russian Musicians," in *Proceedings from the Second International Conference on Sibelius, 1995*, ed. Veijo Murtomäki, Kari Kilpeläinen, and Risto Väisänen (Helsinki: Sibelius Academy, 1998), 174–79.

25 Helena Tyrväinen, "Sibelius at the Paris Universal Exposition of 1900," in *Proceedings from the Second International Conference on Sibelius, 1995*, ed. Veijo Murtomäki, Kari Kilpeläinen, and Risto Väisänen (Helsinki: Sibelius Academy, 1998), 114–28.

26 Edward C. Thaden, "Part One: The Russian Government," in *Russification in the Baltic Provinces and Finland, 1855–1914*, ed. Edward C. Thaden (Princeton, NJ: Princeton University Press, 1981), 28.

27 Tuomo Polvinen, *Imperial Borderland: Bobrikov and the Attempted Russification of Finland 1898–1904*, trans. Steven Huxley (London: Hurst, 1995), 154.

28 The Senate of Finland made internal decisions on Finnish administration with minimal Russian representation. In theory, the Russian Governor-General could preside over its meetings, but in practice he did not often attend.

29 Lundin 1981, 359.

30 Osmo Jussila, "Nationalism and Revolution: Political Dividing Lines in the Grand Duchy of Finland during the Last Years of Russian Rule," *Scandinavian Journal of History* 2 (1977): 291.

31 Details on this intellectual history are given in Michael Branch, "The Academy of Sciences in St. Petersburg as a Centre for the Study of Nationalities in the North-East Baltic," in *National History and Identity: Approaches to the Writing of National History in the North-east Baltic Region—Nineteenth and Twentieth Centuries*, ed. Michael Branch (Helsinki: Finnish Literature Society, 1999), 122–37.

32 Julius Krohn, *Kalevalan toisinnot: Suomen kansallis-epoksen ainekset järjestettyinä sisällyksenä laulupaikkojen mukaan; Jälkimmäinen sarja; Suomen, Aunuksen, Inkerin ja Wiron runot* (Helsinki: Finnish Literature Society, 1888).

33 Julius Krohn, *Suomen Suvun Pakanallinen Jumalanpalvelus* (Helsinki: Finnish Literature Society, 1894).

34 Erkki Pekkilä, "History, Geography, and Diffusion: Ilmari Krohn's Early Influence on the Study of European Folk Music," *Ethnomusicology* 50 (2) (2006): 353–59.

35 Krohn 1945.

36 This meta-narrative is outlined by Markus Mantere, "Writing Out the Nation in Academia: Ilmari Krohn and the National Context of the Beginnings of Musicology in Finland," in *Critical Music Historiography: Probing Canons, Ideologies and Institutions*, ed. Vesa Kurkela and Markus Mantere (Farnham, UK: Ashgate, 2015), 68. Also see Krohn 1945.

37 Juhani Paasivirta, *Finland and Europe: The Period of Autonomy and the International Crises, 1808–1914*, trans. Anthony F. Upton and Sirkka R. Upton (London: C. Hurst, 1981), 194.

CHAPTER 3

1 Nils-Eric Ringbom, *Jean Sibelius: A Master and His Work*, trans. G. I. C. de Courcy (Norman: Oklahoma University Press, 1954), 87.
2 Tawaststjerna 1976, 273–74.
3 Erinn E. Knyt, *Ferruccio Busoni and His Legacy* (Bloomington: Indiana University Press, 2017), chapter 2.
4 For example, see Denis Stevens, "Ferruccio Busoni (1866–1924)," in *The Concerto*, ed. Ralph Hill (Melbourne: Pelican, 1952), 282–88.
5 See Mark Satola, "Ferruccio Busoni, Violin Concerto in D major, op. 35a, KiV 243," AllMusic, http://www.allmusic.com/composition/violin-concerto-in-d-major-op-35a-kiv-243-mc0002373828, accessed August 20, 2017, and Susan Key, "Violin Concerto (Ferruccio Busoni)," https://www.hollywoodbowl.com/musicdb/pieces/4502/violin-concerto, accessed December 16, 2019, who writes that this work "is neither romantic nor modern; it neither breaks new ground nor clings to the past. It acknowledges tradition but within a modern consciousness—something like the attitude Busoni took toward his pianistic interpretations: 'You start from false premises in thinking it is my intention to "modernize" the works. On the contrary, by cleaning them of the dust of tradition, I try to restore them their youth.' And the composer's personal preoccupations are evident throughout: the virtuoso's touch in the work's soaring phrases and idiomatic gestures; the classicist's in its sense of proportion and internal logic.")
6 De Törne 1937, 93.
7 Tawaststjerna 1976, 287.
8 Pekka Kuusisto, interview with Sophia Ramnarine, August 19, 2019.
9 Robin Stowell, *Beethoven: Violin Concerto* (Cambridge: Cambridge University Press, 1998), 12.
10 Kuusisto 2019.
11 Tiilikainen 2004, 68.
12 Tiilikainen 2004, 71.
13 See the facsimile in Virtanen 2014, 236.
14 Tiilikainen 2004, 74.
15 Virtanen 2014, viii.
16 See Veijo Murtomäki, "Sibelius and Finnish-Karelian Folk Music," *Finnish Music Quarterly* 3 (2005): 32–37. Also see Tina K. Ramnarine, "An Encounter with the Other: Sibelius, Folk Music and Nationalism," in *Proceedings from the*

Second International Conference on Sibelius, 1995, ed. Veijo Murtomäki, Kari Kilpeläinen, and Risto Väisänen (Helsinki: Sibelius Academy, 1998), 166–73.

17 Cited in Tawaststjerna 1976, 98.

18 Petri Shemeikka's performance of *Tulen Synty* can be heard on the CD *The Kalevala Heritage: Archive Recordings of Ancient Finnish Songs* (Ondine, ODE 849–2, 1995). The original recording was made using wax cylinder technology.

19 See Murtomäki 2005; Armas Otto Väisänen, "Sibelius ja Kansanmusiikki" [Sibelius and folk music], in *Kalevalaseuran 16 Vuosikirja* [Yearbook 16 of the Kalevala Society] (Porvoo: Werner Söderström Osakeyhtiön Kirjapainossa, 1936), 278.

20 Sibelius 1980 [1896].

21 Murtomäki 2005. The idea of folk modality promoted hegemonic cultural ideologies about Europe's peasants and contributed to the distinction between art and folk music from the eighteenth century onward; see Matthew Gelbart, *The Invention of 'Folk Music' and 'Art Music': Emerging Categories from Ossian to Wagner* (Cambridge: Cambridge University Press, 2007).

22 Karl Ekman, *Jean Sibelius: His Life and Personality* Hong Kong: Hesperides, 2008 [1938]); see chapter 1.

23 Von Bonsdorff 2014, 95.

24 The subject of *Heikki Playing* was Heikki Halonen (Pekka's brother), a student of both Sibelius and Kajanus. He also studied with Auer in St. Petersburg, and he worked as an orchestral violinist in Helsinki; see von Bonsdorff 2014, 154.

25 Letter from Burmester to Sibelius, July 22, 1903, cited in Virtanen 2014, viii.

26 Letter from Sibelius to Burmester, August 8, 1903, cited in Virtanen 2014, viii.

27 Cited in Tawaststjerna 1976, 275.

28 Cited in Virtanen 2014, ix.

29 Cited in Virtanen 2014, ix.

30 Cited in Virtanen 2014, ix.

31 Tawaststjerna 1976, 275.

32 Tawaststjerna 1976, 277.

33 Letter from Burmester to Sibelius, cited in Tawaststjerna 1976, 277.

34 Tawaststjerna 1976, 278.

35 Virtanen 2014, xi.

36 Carpelan had written to Sibelius on October 2, 1903: "I would most warmly recommend sending the piano score to Ysaÿe in Brussels, probably the greatest violin artist today. . . . Through him you would be played everywhere, even in France. . . . [Send] the piano score to Burmester, Ysaÿe, and Marteau. Do not let second-rate virtuosos get hold of the manuscript." Cited in Virtanen 2014, ix.

37 Schoenbaum 2013, 279.

38 However, in a letter to Sibelius of March 13, 1912, Rosa Newmarch asked, "Why are the virtuosi not arguing over who will be the first to perform this

work? . . . In fifteen years it will be a 'classic' like the concertos of Beethoven, Brahms and Tchaikovsky; but I am keen to hear it now. If only Vecsey would play it the next time he comes to London. This boy has great talent." Cited in Philip Ross Bullock, ed., and transl., *The Correspondence of Jean Sibelius and Rosa Newmarch, 1906-1939* (Woodbridge, UK: Boydell, 2011), 145–46.

39 Hubay and his fellow students Joseph Szigeti and Emil Telmányi enjoyed successful concert careers.

40 Cited in Margaret Campbell, *The Great Violinists* (London: Faber & Faber, 2011), 75.

41 Leopold Auer, *My Long Life in Music* (New York: Frederick A. Stokes, 1923), 346.

42 Campbell 2011, 248.

43 Cited in Erik Tawaststjerna, *Sibelius Volume II: 1904-1914*, ed. and trans. Robert Layton (London: Faber & Faber, 1986 [1972]), 147.

44 Cited in Tawaststjerna 1986, 259.

45 Campbell 2011, 248.

46 Tomi Mäkelä, *Jean Sibelius* (Woodbridge, UK: Boydell, 2011), 282.

47 Virtanen 2014, xii.

48 Virtanen 2014, xiv.

49 Cited in Ringbom 1954, 88.

50 Virtanen 2014, x.

51 Virtanen 2014, x.

52 These critiques are cited in Virtanen 2014, x.

53 Cited in Tawaststjerna 1986, 263.

54 Cited in Mäkelä 2011, 287.

55 Cited in Shaffer and Greenwood 1988, 238–39.

56 Shaffer and Greenwood 1988, 238.

57 Shaffer and Greenwood 1988, 239.

58 Shaffer and Greenwood 1988, 249.

59 Shaffer and Greenwood 1988, 238.

60 See Powell's 1914 recording of Sibelius's *Valse Triste* on YouTube, https://www.youtube.com/watch?v=zHz-SWRvdlI, or see audio-visual example 3.1 on the website.

61 Cited in Glenda Dawn Goss, *Jean Sibelius and Olin Downes: Music, Friendship, Criticism* (Boston: Northeastern University Press, 1995), 192–93.

62 Cecil Gray, *Sibelius* (London: Oxford University Press, 1931), 113.

63 Gray 1931, 114–15.

64 Donald Francis Tovey, *Essays in Musical Analysis*, vol. 3, *Concertos* (London: Oxford University Press, 1969 [1936]), 211.

65 Robert Layton, *The Master Musicians: Sibelius* (London: J. M. Dent and Sons, 1965), 103.

66 Layton 1965, 103.

67 Other critics, such as Ringbom, commented on the structural importance of the concerto's most virtuosic passages suggesting there were no merely "acrobatic" details, see Ringbom 1954, 89.

68 Layton 1965, 104.

69 Layton 1965, 105.

70 Layton 1965, 105.

71 Goss 2009, 35.

72 Tiilikainen 2004, 66–67.

73 Virtanen 2014, xii.

74 Jukka-Pekka Saraste, personal communication, August 21, 2019.

75 Virtanen 2014, xiii.

76 Glenda Dawn Goss, "Vienna and the Genesis of *Kullervo*: Durchführung zum Teufel!," in *The Cambridge Companion to Sibelius*, ed. Daniel M. Grimley (Cambridge: Cambridge University Press, 2004), 25–26.

77 Cited in de Törne 1937, 37–38.

78 Carolyn Abbate, "Drastic or Gnostic?" *Critical Inquiry* 30 (3) (2004): 508.

79 Virno 2004, 66.

80 Auer 1980, 80.

CHAPTER 4

1 Banat 2006, 98.

2 Banat 2006, 99.

3 Owe Ronström, "Fiddling with Pasts: From Tradition to Heritage," in *Crossing Over: Fiddle and Dance Studies from around the North Atlantic*, ed. Ian Russell and Anna Kearney Guigné (Aberdeen: Elphinstone Institute, 2010), 266–68.

4 Tina K. Ramnarine, *Ilmatar's Inspirations: Nationalism, Globalization, and the Changing Soundscapes of Finnish Folk Music* (Chicago: University of Chicago Press, 2003), chapter 7.

5 Erkki Salmenhaara, "The Violin Concerto," in *Sibelius Companion*, ed. Glenda D. Goss (Westport, CT: Greenwood, 1996), 113.

6 See "J. SIBELIUS VIOLIN CONCERTO: INTRODUCTION BY IDA HAENDEL," YouTube, https://youtube.com/watch?v=6QZiwHdM-ao, accessed August 20, 2017, or audio-visual example 4.1 on the website.

7 Tovey 1969, 215.

8 Mäkelä 2011, 284.

9 Mäkelä 2011, 290.

10 Ilmari Krohn, ed., *Vanhoja Pelimannisävelmiä* (Hämeenlinna: Suomalaisen Kirjallisuuden Seura, 1975).

11 Einojuhani Rautavaara, *Omakuva* (Porvoo: Werner Söderström Osakeyhtiö, 1989), 116.

12 Marat Gubdallin, "Synthesis of Russian and Western Performing Art Traditions in Violin Music by Ivan Khandoshkin" (PhD diss., University of Oklahoma, 2015), 15.

13 Gubdallin 2015, 32–58.

14 Leopold Auer file, Sibelius Music Archive, hereafter SMA. This archive is at the Sibelius Museum in Turku, Finland. The column was written by Y. S. (possibly Yrjö Suomalainen).

15 Auer 1923, 344–45.

16 An example of Leopold Auer's playing from a ca. 1920 recording of Brahms's Hungarian Dance no. 2 is available on YouTube, https://www.youtube.com/watch?v=QygG9ZFnmfk, accessed August 20, 2017, or see audio-visual example 4.2 on the website.

17 Kopytova 2014; see chapter 4 for a discussion of Heifetz's studies with Nalbandian.

18 Auer 1923, 34.

19 Auer 1923, 59–60.

20 Auer 1923, 63.

21 Auer 1980, 6–7. Auer concluded with the importance of practical demonstration: "In spite of all verbal eloquence a teacher can call to his service, he will never be able to inculcate properly, to compel the pupil to grasp all the delicacies of execution, if he is unable to illustrate, by means of the violin itself, whatever he asks the pupil to do."

22 Tovey 1969, 106.

23 Tovey 1969, 109.

24 A documentary about Auer and his students is available in two parts in English on YouTube, https://www.youtube.com/watch?v=OJIK-Gq29J8 (part 1) and https://www.youtube.com/watch?v=R2QNZNezS-s (part 2), or see audio-visual examples 4.3 and 4.4 on the website. This documentary is also available in two parts in the original Russian on YouTube, https://www.youtube.com/watch?v=A9wXYoueIRM (part 1) and https://www.youtube.com/watch?v=9Lbfpg2HQpQ (part 2), or see audio-visual examples 4.5 and 4.6 on the website.

25 Auer 1980, 93.

26 It is possible to gain an impression of Wilhelm Burmester's playing through a 1909 recording of his arrangement of a sarabande by Handel. See "Willy Burmester, Violin Hendel-Burmester: Sarabande," YouTube, https://www.youtube.com/watch?v=zrJdgYqupHY, accessed October 16, 2019, or see audio-visual example 4.7 on the website.

27 The correspondence is available on the Tchaikovsky Research website at http://en.tchaikovsky-research.net/pages/Willy_Burmester, accessed June 4, 2017.

28 Auer 1923, 148.

29 Auer 1923, 150.

30 Auer 1923, 154–55.

31 Auer 1923, 157.

32 Mark Slobin, *Fiddler on the Move: Exploring the Klezmer World* (Oxford: Oxford University Press, 2000), 118.

33 Yale Strom, *The Book of Klezmer: The History, the Music, the Folklore* (Chicago: A Cappella, 2002).

34 Kopytova 2014, 15.

35 Saraste, 2019.

36 David Oistrakh's 1966 live performance of the Sibelius violin concerto with the Moscow Radio Symphony Orchestra conducted by Gennady Rozhdesetvensky is available on YouTube, https://www.youtube.com/watch?v=LQmskA9rvwU, accessed February 19, 2020, or see audio-visual example 4.8 on the website.

37 James Loeffler, *The Most Musical Nation: Jews and Culture in the Late Russian Empire* (New Haven, CT: Yale University Press, 2010), chapter 3.

38 Joshua S. Walden, *Sounding Authentic: The Rural Miniature and Musical Modernism* (Oxford: Oxford University Press, 2014), 139.

39 Walden 2014, 75–80.

40 Kopytova 2014, 67–68.

41 Walden 2014.

42 Auer 1923, 9.

43 Alexandra M. Eddy, "American Violin Method-Books and European Teachers, Geminiani to Spohr," *American Music* 8 (2) (1990): 167–209.

44 Auer 1980, 94. The list of some of the violinists who performed in Finland following the premiere of Sibelius's violin concerto was compiled from scrutinizing materials in the Sibelius Music Archive, Turku.

45 Auer 1980, 77.

46 Auer 1980, 80.

47 Auer 1980, 80.

48 Auer 1980, 75.

49 Stefan Knapik, "The Master(ed) Violinist: Carl Flesch's Pedagogical Treatise and Memoirs," *Music and Letters* 96, no, 4 (2015): 579.

50 This theory coincided with Finnish visual artists using color to depict an inner voice, as well as with vocal metaphors in commentary on Russian Jewish folk music, according to which the voice was "as a conduit conveying interior sentiments to the outside world." Walden 2014, 146.

51 Bronstein 2016, 25.

52 Bronstein, 2016, 119.

53 Bronstein 2016, 119.

54 Bronstein 2016, 119.

55 Bronstein 2016, 130.

56 Bronstein 2016, 134.

57 Parlow is cited by the anonymous author of "Leopold Auer: The Man, His Methods and Ideals in Teaching," *Musical Standard*, June 10, 1911, 354–57.

58 Carl Flesch, *The Memoirs of Carl Flesch*, trans. Hans Keller (London: Rockliff, 1957), 69.

59 Flesch 1957, 69.

60 Her 1924 recorded performance of Brahms's Hungarian Dance number 4 is available on YouTube, https://www.youtube.com/watch?v=RY-wpGthLmY, accessed June 25, 2017, or see audio-visual example 4.9 on the website.

61 Flesch 1957, 338.

62 Henry Roth, *Master Violinists in Performance* (Neptune City, NJ: Paganiniana, 1982), 248.

63 Roth 1982, 248.

64 Antero Karttunen, *Anja Ignatius – Sibeliuksen tulkitsija* (Juva: WS Bookwell Oy, 2004), 282.

65 SMA, Kerttu Wanne files.

CHAPTER 5

1 Jascha Heifetz, *Sibelius Violin Concerto in D Minor op. 47*, London Philharmonic Orchestra conducted by Thomas Beecham, re-released 2000 by Naxos Historical Records, Catalogue no. 8.110938, originally recorded in 1935. Available on YouTube at https://www.youtube.com/watch?v=-yvy9lS5DC4&list=RD-yvy9lS5DC4&index=1, accessed April 24, 2019, or see audio-visual example 5.1 on the website.

2 Flesch 1957, 335–36.

3 Flesch 1957, 337.

4 Tossy Spivakovsky with the London Symphony Orchestra conducted by Tauno Hannikainen (Everest SDBR 3045, 1959).

5 Mark Katz, "Portamento and the Phonograph Effect," *Journal of Musicological Research* 25 (3/4) (2006): 211–32.

6 Ayke Agus, *Heifetz as I Knew Him* (Portland, OR: Amadeus, 2001), 145.

7 Agus 2001, 145.

8 See Jascha Heifetz's restored 1951 live recording of the Sibelius violin concerto with the New York Philharmonic on YouTube, https://www.youtube.com/watch?v=HWnlvq5oAG8, accessed April 24, 2019, or see audio-visual example 5.2 on the website.

9 Flesch 1957, 173.

10 Flesch 1957, 254.

11 Archie Mayo, dir., *They Shall Have Music* (Samuel Goldwyn Productions, 1939).

12 Peter Rosen, dir., *God's Fiddler: Jascha Heifetz* (Peter Rosen Productions, 2011).

13 Goss 1995, 130.

14 Goss 1995, 105.

15 Goss 1995, 98–129.

16 Stefan Knapik, "Vitalistic Discourses of Violin Pedagogy in the Early Twentieth Century," *19th-Century Music* 38 (2) (2014): 169–90.

17 Cited on the Maud Powell Foundation website, http://www.maudpowell.org/home/MaudPowell/Recordings/Pioneer.aspx, accessed August 20, 2017.

18 Flesch 1957, 292.

19 Anja Ignatius, "Violin Concerto", *Historical Sibelius Recordings*, with the Berlin Municipal Orchestra conducted by Armas Järnefelt, recorded 1943 Finlandia, FACD 810, 1991. Available on YouTube, https://www.youtube.com/watch?v=esDbR3-QKZE, accessed August 9, 2019, or see audio-visual example 5.3 on the website.

20 See Ignatius's 1952 performance of the Sibelius violin concerto with the Radio Symphony Orchestra on YouTube, https://www.youtube.com/watch?v=S3wzwY5oRoo, accessed August 9, 2019, or see audio-visual example 5.4 on the website.

21 Heimo Haitto, *Heimo Haitto Plays Sibelius*, with the Finnish Radio Symphony Orchestra, conducted by Paavo Berglund, recorded 1964, Finlandia Classics FINCLA 2, 2013.

22 Karttunen 2004, 284.

23 Saraste 2019.

24 Vilde Frang, *Sibelius's Violin Concerto and Humoresques and Prokofiev's Violin Concerto no. 1*, with WDR Sinfonieorchester conducted by Thomas Sondergard, EMI Classics, 2010.

25 Ida Haendel, *Woman with Violin: The Autobiography of Ida Haendel* (London: Victor Gollancz, 1970), 192.

26 Haendel 1970, 192.

27 Paul Cohen, dir., *I Am the Violin* (MOONDOCS, 2004), available on YouTube, https://www.youtube.com/watch?v=2fARPbGGbtE, accessed June 25, 2017, or see audio-visual example 5.5 on the website.

28 According to Mark D. Brownell in a review of the CD, available on AllMusic at http://www.allmusic.com/album/sibelius-violin-concerto-elgar-violin-concerto-mw0001877952, accessed June 28, 2017. The CD is *Testament: Ida Haendel Plays Sibelius and Elgar*, City of Birmingham Symphony Orchestra conducted by Simon Rattle, BBC recording of a live 1993 performance, Testament SBT 1444, 1996.

29 Haendel 1970, 14.

30 Haendel 1970, 90.

31 Flesch 1957, 53.

32 Haendel 1970, 90.

33 Haendel 1970, 150.

34 Erkki Salmenhaara, *Jean Sibelius Violin Concerto* (Wilhelmshaven, Germany: Florian Noetzel Verlag, 1996), 34.

35 Salmenhaara 1996, 34.

36 Haendel 1970, 156.

37 Goss 1995, 109.

38 Haendel 1970, 156.

39 Haendel 1970, 156.

40 Haendel 1970, 157.

41 Haendel 1970, 256.

42 Haendel 1970, 237.

43 Haendel makes these comments in a video about Sibelius's violin concerto; see audio-visual example 4.1 on the website.

44 Heimo Haitto, *Maailmalla* (Helsinki: Kirjayhtymä, 1976), 7, my translation.

45 Haitto 1976, 9–19.

46 Haitto 1976, 27, my translation and paraphrasing.

47 Andrew L. Stone, dir., *There's Magic in Music* (Paramount Pictures; first released under the title *The Hard-Boiled Canary*, 1941), available on YouTube, https://www.youtube.com/watch?v=HS9fOlNVgVI, accessed June 25, 2017, or see audio-visual example 5.6 on the website.

48 Toivo Särkkä, dir., *Pikku Pelimannista Viulun Kuninkaaksi* [The little fiddler becomes the king of the violin] (Suomen Filmiteollisuus, 1949).

49 See the biography on Jukka-Pekka Saraste's website, http://jukkapekkasaraste. com/about/youth/, accessed September 7, 2016. Saraste has also commented on Lahti as a significant link between Finnish and Russian music: "I also started music studies in Vyborg's Music School, which after the war was situated in Lahti. It was full of teachers and real cultural personalities coming from Russia. . . . By advice of Boris Sirpo I started my violin lessons under Heimo Haitto and played piano under Lea Terno. Later I continued my violin studies in Naum Levin's class. They all had come from Vyborg or from Russia through Vyborg to Lahti." Quoted on the Sinfonia Lahti website, http://www. sinfonialahti.fi/ajankohtaista/uutiset2008/en_GB/st_petersburg/, accessed September 11, 2016.

50 Heimo Haitto, *Viuluniekka kulkurina* [The fiddler as a hobo] (Helsinki: Tammi, 1994).

51 Anneli Mäkelä-Alitalo, "Haitto, Heimo (1925–1999)," trans. Wastie Oliver, National Biography of Finland website, http://www.kansallisbiografia.fi/english/?id=8136, accessed September 7, 2016.

52 A photograph of Sibelius shaking Sirpo's hand following the concert is available on the Sibelius website at http://www.sibelius.fi/english/elamankaari/sib_viimeiset.htm, accessed September 7, 2016.

53 SuviSirkku Talas, ed., *Rakas äitini! Armas, Eero, Arvid ja Kasper Järnefeltin sekä Aino Sibeliuksen kirjeitä äidilleen Elizabeth Järnefeltille, 1879–1928* (Hämeenlinna: Karisto Oy, 2014), 330–31.

54 See, for example, two comments on the Violinist.com website, http://www.violinist.com/discussion/archive/8303/ and http://www.violinist.com/discussion/archive/12465/, accessed August 20, 2017.

CHAPTER 6

1 File FM 4/2/76 on Sibelius, Menuhin's writings and articles, Menuhin Archive, Royal Academy of Music, London

2 Tiilikainen 2004, 76.

3 Cited in Virtanen 2014, ix.

4 Joseph Kerman, *Concerto Conversations* (Cambridge, MA: Harvard University Press, 1999), 68.

5 Kalevi Aho, *Violin Concerto* in the liner notes to a CD recording of Aho's Violin Concerto, BIS-CD-396, 1989, no pagination.

6 Saraste, 2019.

7 For example, Veijo Murtomäki, "The Responsibility of an Artist," *Finnish Music Quarterly* 2015 (1–2), available online at http://www.fmq.fi/2015/04/the-responsibility-of-an-artist/, accessed June 3, 2017.

8 Huttunen 2004, 18.

9 Hegel 1977, 68.

10 See "Viktoria Mullova | The Violin Channel Masterclass | Surrendering Yourself to Concert Nerves," YouTube, https://www.youtube.com/watch?v=3xLShADpKTY, accessed August 20, 2017.

11 See "Finnish Folk Music—Pekka Kuusisto Home Video—July 2017 (Philharmonia Orchestra)," YouTube, https://www.youtube.com/watch?v=mDpujmHNvUo, accessed August 20, 2017.

12 See "Pekka Kuusisto's Hilarious Proms encore—My Darling Is Beautiful," YouTube, https://www.youtube.com/watch?v=gpN2k5zz810, accessed August 20, 2017.

13 See the Meidän Festivaali website, https://meidanfestivaali.fi/eng/, accessed August 29, 2019.

14 For example, see "Ekki Melartin—Violin Concerto in D-minor, Op. 60 (1913), YouTube, https://www.youtube.com/watch?v=qY8xcUcaWjE, accessed August 20, 2017, a performance with John Storgårds as soloist with the Tampere Philharmonic Orchestra conducted by Leif Segerstam.

15 See Satu Kahila, "First Performances 1977–," YLE website, August 25, 2014, https://yle.fi/aihe/artikkeli/2014/08/25/first-performances-1977, accessed August 20, 2017. Many concertos for other instruments are also listed.

16 See "Record Amount of Applicants for 11th Jean Sibelius Violin Competition," on the UniArts Helsinki website at https://www.uniarts.fi/en/newsroom/enn%C3%A4tysm%C3%A4%C3%A4r%C3%A4-ilmoittautui-sibelius-viulukilpailuun, accessed August 20, 2017.

17 Levas 1972, 8

18 Chris Salter, *Entangled: Technology and the Transformation of Performance* (Cambridge, MA: MIT Press, 2010), 32.

19 Immanuel Kant, *Anthropology from a Pragmatic Point of View*, ed. Robert B. Louden (Cambridge: Cambridge University Press 2006 [1798]), 169.

20 Auer 1980, 66.

21 Levas 1972, 49.

22 Levas 1972, 49.

23 Aaron S. Allen, "'Fatto di Fiemme': Stradivari's Violins and the Musical Trees of the Paneveggio," in *Invaluable Trees: Cultures of Nature, 1660–1830*, ed. Laura Auricchio, Elizabeth Heckendorn Cook, and Giulia Pacini (Oxford: Volaire Foundation, 2012), 301–15.

24 For these instrument histories see the Tarisio website at tarisio.com, accessed June 3, 2017.

25 Allen 2012, 314.

26 Cited in Kari Kilpeläinen, *Jean Sibelius: Ainola, Järvenpää* (Porvoo: WSOY, 1995), 16.

27 Bernie Krause, *The Great Animal Orchestra: Finding the Origins of Music in the World's Wild Places* (New York: Little, Brown, 2012), 4.

INDEX

Herder, Johann Gottfried, 21, 40
heritage, 35, 117, 129n21
Hill and Son Company, 106
Hřímalý, Bohuslav, 32
Hubay, Jenö, 55
Hämeenlinna, 11, 13–14, 43

Ignatius, Anja, 66, 79, 87
  recording of Sibelius violin
    concerto, 96–98
imperialism, Russian, 12
industrialization, 11, 13
inspiration, 6–7, 18, 75, 90, 110
interpretation, 10, 17, 68, 83, 100,
    117, 119
  ecological, 11, 129n21
  of Sibelius violin concerto, 66–67,
    69, 79, 90–92, 95, 97–99, 101,
    108, 116

Jalas, Jussi, 5
Jalas, Satu, 14
Jean Sibelius Works, 9
Joachim, Joseph, 29, 44, 50,
    55–56, 75–76
Järnefelt, Armas, 31, 35, 97, 107

Kajanus, Robert, 18–19, 29, 30–36, 54,
    90, 92–93
Kalevala, 5, 19–20, 34–35, 38,
    40–41, 48
Kant, Immanuel, 118
kantele, 48
Karelianism, 34–35
Kavakos, Leonidas, 9, 108
Khandoshkin, Ivan
    Yefstafyevich, 30, 73
Kivi, Aleksis, 38
klezmer, 11, 77–79, 92
Koussevitzky, Sergei, 71, 93
Kreisler, Fritz, 53, 80

Kreutzer, Rudolphe, 14, 45, 74
Krohn, Ilmari, 1, 40–41, 72
Krohn, Julius, 40
Krohn, Kaarle, 40
Kuusisto, Pekka, 9, 45, 113–15

labor, 13, 23–24, 67–68, 88
  compositional, 5
  of virtuosity, 2–3, 23–24, 110
  of women virtuosos, 86, 89
  political potential of, 24
  wage, 24
Lake Tuusula, 7, 49, 113
Launis, Armas, 41, 48
Leino, Eino, 49
Levander, Gustaf, 13
Levas, Santeri, 6, 117–19
Lienau, Robert, 53, 56, 66–67
Liszt, Franz, 13
Lully, Jean-Baptiste, 69
luthier, 4, 119–20
Lönnrot, Elias, 19, 40

Marx, Karl, 23, 25, 110
Massart, Lambert Joseph, 30
Mazas, Jacques Féréol, 14
Melartin, Erkki, 115
Mendelssohn, Felix, 17, 29, 74
Menuhin, Yehudi, 99, 100, 103, 109
Merikanto, Oskar, 57
method books, 82
  Méthode de Violon, 14
  *The Art of Bowing: Variations on a
    Theme by Corelli*, 73
metronome mark, 66
military band, 12
Mozart, Wolfgang Amadeus, 28
Mullova, Viktoria, 4, 113, 115
music history, 28
  ecological, 118
musicology, Finnish, 40–41, 129n21